ENTRÉE TO

ENTRÉE TO HALKIDIKI

GREECE'S SECRET PARADISE

Chris McLoughlin

Quiller Press

First published 1995 by Quiller Press Ltd
46 Lillie Road, London SW6 1TN

Copyright 1995 © Chris McLoughlin
Illustrations and maps: © 1995 Quiller Press Ltd
Front cover: Tim Jaques
Illustrations: Emma Mcleod-Johnstone
Maps: Pete Welford
Design & Production in association with
Book Production Consultants plc, Cambridge

ISBN 1 899163 02 6

All rights reserved. No part of this book may be
reproduced or transmitted, in any form or by
any means, without permission of the publishers.

Photoset by Rowland Phototypesetting Ltd
Bury St Edmunds, Suffolk
Printed in Great Britain by
Cox & Wyman Ltd, Reading, Berks.

Contents

Foreword   vii
Entrée to Halkidiki   ix
Acknowledgements   xii
Introduction   1
Maps 4

HALKIDIKI

Tips for beginners   8
   When to go – The language – Money – Local geography – Transport – Walking – Food and drink – Beaches – Festivals – What to bring back
A brief history   36
   In the mountains   40
   Thessaloniki   45
   Kassandra peninsula   58
   Sithonia peninsula   99
   Athos peninsula   115

Bus timetables   129
Index   131

Foreword

As the President of the Halkidiki Hotel Association, I am delighted that, at long last, there is an authoritative and thoroughly readable guide book to this beautiful region of Greece.

The holiday brochures describe Halkidiki as dramatically beautiful. They are not exaggerating. The three peninsulas which comprise Halkidiki: Kassandra, Sithonia and Athos, each have their own distinct charm and character and all offer holidaymakers a taste of real Greece in the most stunning setting imaginable. In addition, only 2½% of the region has been developed and there are no rivers or industry to cause pollution, so it remains unspoilt.

Each year we are welcoming more British visitors, which we are delighted about, and most UK tour operators feature programmes to Halkidiki offering a wide range of holidays to suit all tastes and budgets. We have deluxe resort hotels of the highest standard, we have small, friendly, family-run pensions, we have tavernas, bars and nightlife and we have deserted beaches, peace and solitude. In short, we can offer visitors whatever they want for a perfect holiday.

We also have a beautiful and fascinating city on our doorstep, with excellent shops, a wealth of musuems and churches and a famous market. Thessaloniki is Greece's second city and is just an hour away from Halkidiki, making it the ideal choice for a day trip. However, for lovers of good food and nightlife we recommend a slightly longer stay in the city as Thessaloniki is renowned for having the best bouzouki bars in the whole of Greece! In 1997 Thessaloniki will be Europe's City of Culture.

Until now there has never been a complete guide to Halkidiki covering all aspects of the region. 'Entrée to Halkidiki' fits the bill exactly and offers a wealth of information on our historical and archaeological sites, gives advice on how to get around using local transport, recommends our finest restaurants, instructs on how to find a 'secret' beach (of which we have many!) and, most importantly, imparts plenty of useful 'local' knowledge.

It is this 'local' knowledge which makes the guide so eminently readable and we hope that visitors to Halkidiki will be encouraged to explore as much as they can during their stay.

With over 300 miles of unspoilt coastline, with some of the finest sandy beaches in Europe, Halkidiki is deservedly popular as a relaxing sun, sea and sand destination, but we are keen to help our visitors move away from the beaches to discover the region's many other attractions on foot, by bicycle or by local bus.

Come to Halkidiki and read the guide, or read the guide and then come to Halkidiki. Whichever way you do it, we look forward to welcoming you in Halkidiki where you can discover your own 'secret paradise'.

Andreas Andreadis
President
HALKIDIKI HOTEL ASSOCIATION

ENTRÉE TO HALKIDIKI

While the formula is basically the same as for the other Entrée Guides, a large allowance has to be made for the fact that Greece is very different from the other countries covered by the series. As before, hotels and restaurants are put into three categories: Luxury (L), Medium (M) and Simple (S). The criterion is, as always, value for money with a smile.

There are half a dozen rather smart hotels, with marble floors, air conditioning and all other mod. cons. including a high standard of service. On the nearby beaches, there will be ample facilities for watersports, sunbeds and parasols, all at an extra charge, although the poolside loungers and umbrellas are free. These hotels are very comfortable indeed and most of them are on a large scale, with hundreds of rooms and often lavish surroundings. Although their restaurants will include some local dishes, and several have à la carte tavernas specialising in Greek cuisine, plus organised 'Greek evenings', in general they tend to have more of an international than Greek flavour. In the smaller or less luxurious establishments, you will often find a more intimate and easy-going atmosphere, but without the full range of facilities the larger ones can offer. You will usually get a simple but clean and adequate room, almost always with a balcony, a decent shower and loo and sometimes a fridge and/or cooking rings. Many hotels have a pool, and most a bar and snack bar, plus somewhere to serve breakfast.

Without exception, I have always found hotel staff friendly and genuinely anxious to be helpful, provided you don't ask the impossible. In the height of summer, your bedroom may well be very hot at night, unless you have booked one with air conditioning, and it's up to you to take precautions against mosquitos. I have heard of holidaymakers blaming hotel staff for both these inconveniences, which is hardly fair.

With a few exceptions, the hotel owners of Halkidiki have learned from the mistakes made in other parts of the country, and they have built very few of the ugly great concrete blocks which disfigure the landscape in parts of Rhodes or Corfu, for example. Even where the exteriors are none too beautiful, the decor inside is usually much better and you can't hear every word said in the room next door as you can in some of the ticky-tacky constructions elsewhere.

As virtually no one travels independently to Halkidiki, I have avoided mentioning many of the excellent hotels which are not available through British tour operators. Some of those included here, especially the larger ones, will have a mixed clientele of various nationalities, others will be exclusively occupied by Brits. One positive aspect of this kind of demarcation is that you will always find staff who speak good English, although the same will not always be true in tavernas and bars.

As far as restaurants and tavernas are concerned, it won't take you long to realise that Luxury category establishments are pretty thin on the ground, and even Medium is not all that common. There is usually nothing much wrong with the establishments in the Simple category, however. Unless you go very early or late in the season, you will almost always be sitting outside, under trees, canvas umbrellas or some kind of awning providing shade, so decor is relatively unimportant. It's not at all unusual for tables or chairs to be a bit wobbly because they're on an uneven surface, and while you may get a fresh tablecloth, it's much more likely that a new plastic one will be brought and fixed over the ordinary cloth with clips or lengths of elastic. Your cutlery will normally appear in the bread basket, occasionally wrapped in a napkin or sometimes with a Cellophane pack containing paper napkin, toothpick and freshen-up tissue in a sealed sachet. There's really no need to book, and in fact in most places they would probably think you were crazy if you tried. The only exception might be if you were going to dine late with a large party at one of the L category tavernas and then only at weekends in July or August. Otherwise, a table will always be found for you somehow, even if the place is frantic.

While service with a smile is the norm almost everywhere in Halkidiki, there are a few exceptions. Very occasionally, this may be down to genuine surliness, but it's much more likely to be because all the customers have arrived at once and the staff are rushed off their feet. The differences can be dramatic depending on when you go. In July and August, thousands of Greek people from Thessaloniki and the surrounding areas swarm into the resorts of Halkidiki, especially at weekends. They all tend to want to eat and drink at the same time, and hotel, restaurant and bar staff will often tell you that they are far more demanding and impatient than holidaymakers from other countries. At other times, especially in June and September, everywhere is very much quieter, and people have more time to chat and make a fuss of you. In May and October, things can be very quiet indeed, and for many visitors this is a positive advantage, but you need to be aware that the place will not be in full swing. Exactly when individual establishments open and close for the season will often depend on how much redecorating there is to be done, the weather, how many customers are about or any number of other imponderables.

Another difference between this and other Entrée guides is a certain vagueness about opening and closing times each day. Apart from some places in Thessaloniki and Porto Carras which operate according to pre-set timetables, these are flexible in the extreme. Individual entries list these times when required, but otherwise, tavernas and other eateries are likely to be open when you get up, and still open when you go to bed, unless you're a real night owl. From about mid-June to the beginning of September, this is virtually universal, but either side of those dates some places won't be open at all or may have a partially restricted menu. The good news, though, is that you'll never be short of somewhere nice to eat and drink, whatever the season.

Greece has been described as 'an approximate society', and it seems to me to sum up the place perfectly. Apart from buses and ferries, which do normally run to a timetable, punctuality or precision about time in general is not considered much of a virtue in Greece. Unless you are committed to eating between certain hours in your hotel, you may as well leave your watches in your suitcase and get used to doing things when you feel like it instead of by the clock. It's a great feeling once you get the hang of it!

Halkidiki promotes itself as the 'secret paradise of Greece', and although this is no longer literally true, it's still appropriate. Inside some of the larger resort complexes this may not always be obvious, but you don't have to move far to find peaceful walks, half-empty beaches and friendly people only too willing to welcome you to their beautiful part of Greece. Even the most commercial resorts have a unique personality, all a little different from each other, and every one worth getting to know better.

Acknowledgements

Many people gave me valuable help and advice while I was working on this guide, and I owe particular thanks to Dr Andreas Andreadis and his colleagues of the Halkidiki Hotel Association. I stayed in some truly delightful hotels, many of which are mentioned in the following pages. However, I should also like to express my appreciation to the management and staff of the Philoxenia Bungalows in Psakoudia, the Mount Athos in Ierissos and the Dolphin Beach in Possidi. At the time of writing, they are all exclusively contracted with German tour operators, but should the situation change, I would not hesitate to recommend them to British holidaymakers.

I could never have written the book without the patient help of Maria Kyrlidou of the Halkidiki Hotel Association, who made endless arrangements and answered interminable questions, as well as introducing me to many fascinating places and people. I must also thank Mrs Lydia Carras, who welcomed me with such hospitality and opened my eyes to so many aspects of Greek life and culture. My thanks too to Simi Pasalidou of Porto Carras for organising my visits there, and for her company during my stays. I learned a lot about the food of the region from Rosemary Barron, author of *Flavours of Greece* (Ebury Press 1992) and especially from her editor Pat Herbert, who was able to enlighten me about so many of the dishes we ate, and who also translated the information on the walks.

Many holidaymakers with whom I spoke while doing my research took time to tell me of their experiences – my thanks to you all. Finally, my thanks to Doug Goodman who first suggested that I should write this book.

INTRODUCTION

Halkidiki is not, as many people imagine, yet another Greek island, but a three-pronged peninsula located some 69 km to the south of the country's second city Thessaloniki (or Salonika). It is part of the area of northern Greece known as Macedonia, where Alexander the Great is still remembered enthusiastically as the local hero. Nearly all of the 80,000 or so British visitors who come here every year arrive by air, then transfer to the resort of their choice by coach.

In theory, there's nothing to stop you booking a flight to Thessaloniki airport and making your way by bus, taxi or

Houses with red-tiled roofs and flower-filled gardens are typical of Halkidiki.

hire car to Halkidiki, but very few people actually do this, so facilities for the independent traveller are less abundant than elsewhere in Greece. Out of the high season, you could almost certainly find rooms in hotels, and there are simple rooms in village houses available to tourists who turn up on spec, but finding accommodation could be more difficult in high season. At weekends and throughout July and August, rooms are scarce because of the influx of Greeks pouring into the resorts from Thessaloniki and surrounding areas. Until a few years ago, the area's many civilised campsites were popular with visitors who came by road, but the effective closure of the most practical route through what used to be Yugoslavia has reduced the demand dramatically. For those who can spare longer than the standard fortnight, there is the option of driving to Ancona or Brindisi in Italy, where you can get ferries to the Greek mainland. From the Ionian sea ports, you can drive across the Peloponnese to Halkidiki. This trip is not for the faint-hearted, however. It would take a minimum of five days, allowing for overnight stays, and you could expect to pay quite a lot in petrol.

Anyone who knows Greece only from the popular holiday islands further south will be stunned by the lush green of the landscape of Halkidiki. The whole region is heavily wooded with pines and olive groves, while inland there are vineyards and fertile farmland in a patchwork of colour. Although the fields themselves fade to a yellowish-brown by the end of the summer, the trees and vines retain their life and colour right through the season. The most obvious attraction for holidaymakers is Halkidiki's 500 km of beaches, where the sea is unbelievably clear and bluer than even the most unconvincing postcard. There are no rivers in Halkidiki, which is said to be why the sea is so clear and clean. Another real plus is that you won't find sewage or rubbish in the sea or on the beaches – although you may come across jellyfish now and then – and thirty-two of the beaches have been awarded the European Union's Blue Flag for quality and cleanliness (see page 31).

The 'prefecture' or administrative area known as Halkidiki covers some 2,945 square kilometres, stretching from the mountainous area in the north down to the tips of the three peninsulas – Kassandra, Sithonia and Athos. While Athos – or Agion Oros, the Holy Mountain – is physically part of Halkidiki, it is quite separate in other respects. It is a self-governing entity under the exclusive control of the Orthodox monks who live and work in its many monasteries, and has its own border controls.

Although a certain number of visitors are allowed in each year, you have to get special permission in advance – involving much form-filling – but even this limited access is not permitted to females. Since its first charter was written (on ram skin!) in 972 AD, no woman nor indeed any female creature has been permitted to set foot in the State of Athos.

The main holiday resorts are spaced around Kassandra, the most commercialised 'prong', Sithonia, the centre 'prong' and the upper part of Athos, with others along the coastlines linking them. Each peninsula has its own, slightly different character, and although none of the resorts is more than a big village, some are quite small and relatively undeveloped.

To the north of the coastal region the country becomes mountainous, and there are charming inland towns and villages which are well worth a visit. Most of the roads are very good and uncrowded except at the height of the season, although as you go higher the twists and turns can be a bit hair-raising as you look down on the countryside spread out far below.

Some 90 minutes by road to the north-west of Halkidiki is the city of Thessaloniki. It's not actually part of the prefecture of Halkidiki, but it is well worth visiting at least once. Its museums are relatively small-scale, but very well done, and even if you don't normally go in for that kind of thing, it's worth making an exception to see the finds from Vergina – the tomb of Philip of Macedon, Father of Alexander the Great – at the archaeological museum. As well as plenty of stylish shops, you'll also find a good choice of cafés and tavernas where you can sit and watch the world go by.

Although the area as a whole has a rich and interesting history, few people go there purely in search of classic temple ruins or major archaeological sites. Nevertheless, there are a number of smaller sites worth seeing, and they have the advantage of not being overrun with tourists nor 'restored' by enthusiastic but misguided archaeologists. They tend to be located in the middle of very attractive countryside, and are often worth visiting if only for the view.

Further afield, you can visit sites such as Pella, the birthplace of Alexander the Great and Vergina where his father Philip was buried, and Meteora – a stunning lunar landscape of strange mountain peaks. Most tour operators run excursions to these destinations, but to visit Meteora you have to be prepared for a very early start and late return, as well as many hours of coach travel.

HALKIDIKI

Maps

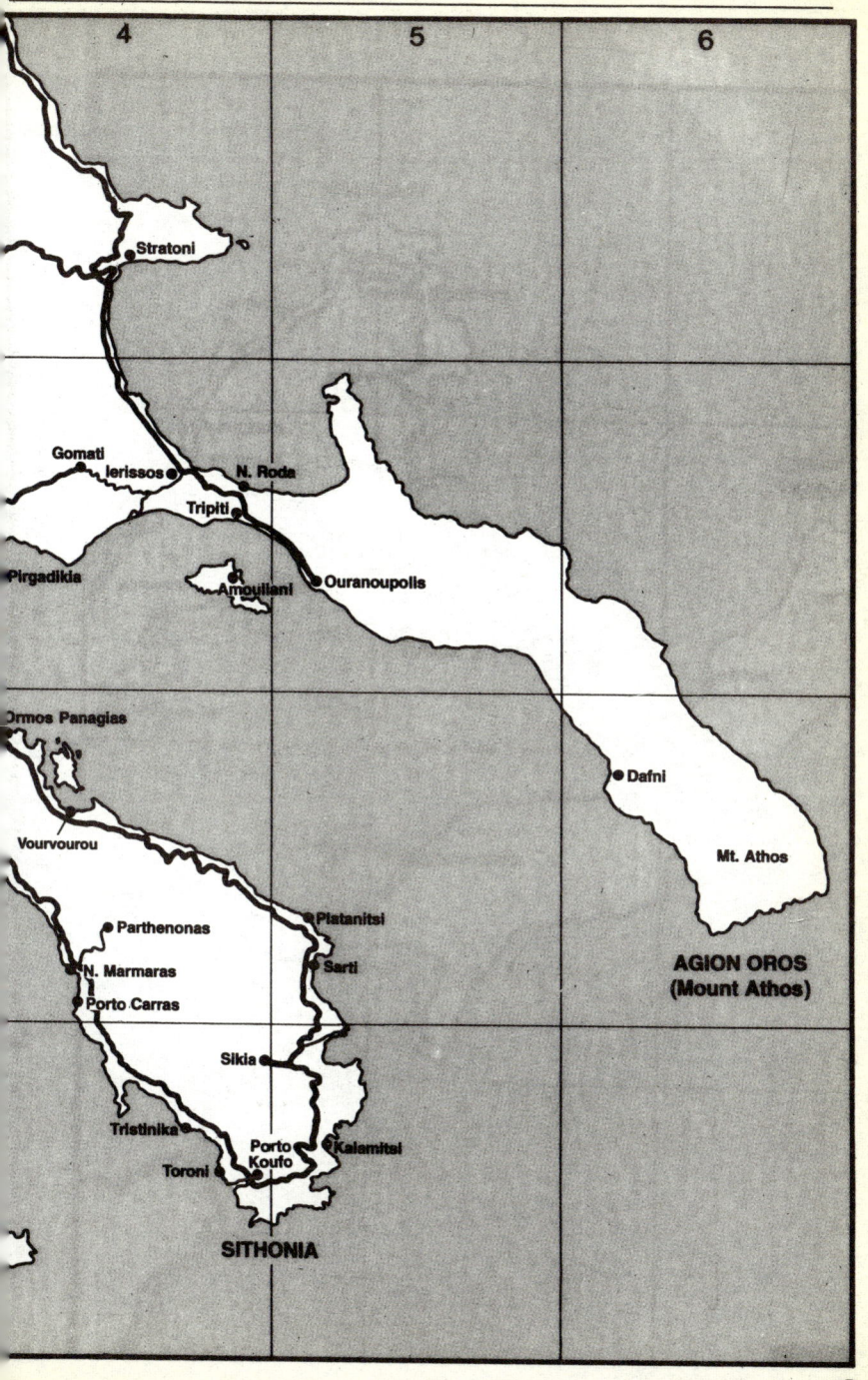

SITHONIA

AGION OROS
(Mount Athos)

- Stratoni
- Gomati
- Ierissos
- N. Roda
- Tripiti
- Pirgadikia
- Amouliani
- Ouranoupolis
- Ormos Panagias
- Vourvourou
- Parthenonas
- Platanitsi
- N. Marmaras
- Sarti
- Porto Carras
- Sikia
- Tristinika
- Porto Koufo
- Kalamitsi
- Toroni
- Dafni
- Mt. Athos

THESSALONIKI

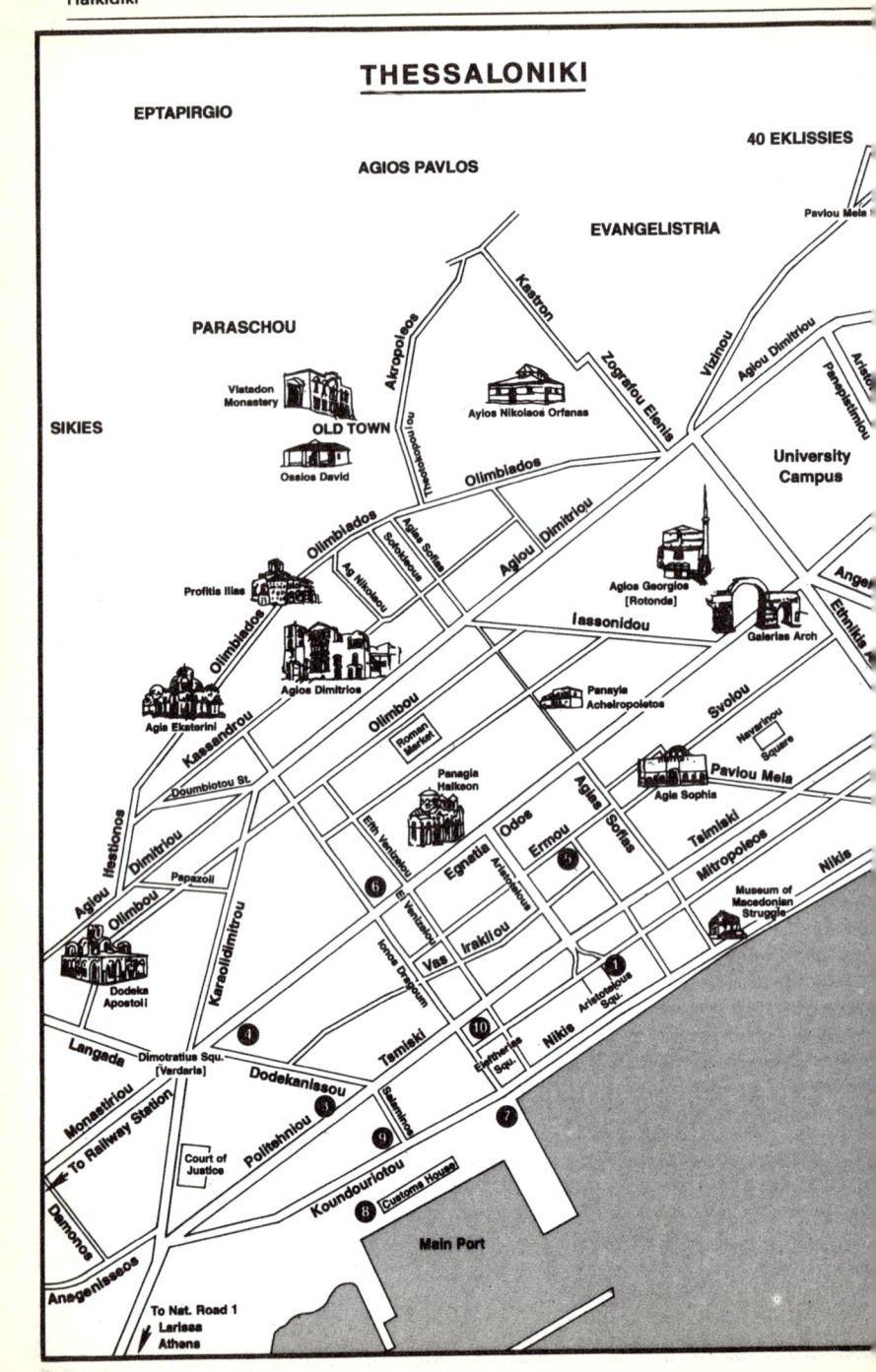

Maps

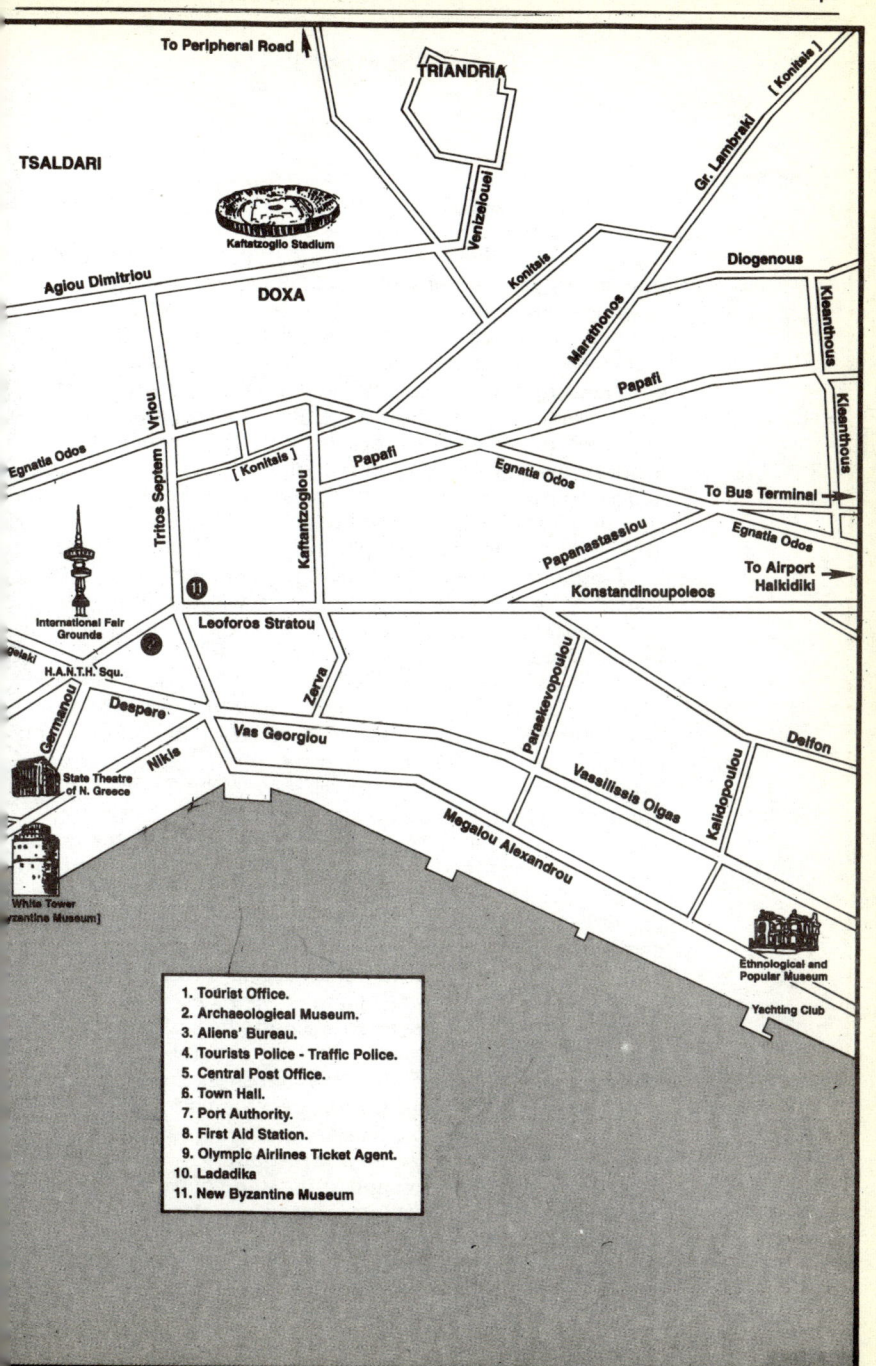

TSALDARI

To Peripheral Road

TRIANDRIA

Kaftatzoglio Stadium

DOXA

Agiou Dimitriou

Venizelouel

Gr. Lambraki [Konitais]

Konitsis

Diogenous

Marathonos

Kleanthous

Papafi

Kleanthous

Egnatia Odos

Vriou

Tritos Septem

[Konitais]

Papafi

Egnatia Odos

To Bus Terminal

Kaftantzoglou

Papanastassiou

Egnatia Odos

⑪

Konstandinoupoleos

To Airport
Halkidiki

International Fair Grounds

Leoforos Stratou

H.A.N.T.H. Squ.

Zerva

Paraskevopoulou

Despare

Germanou

Delfon

Nikis

Vas Georgiou

Vassilissis Olgas

Kallidopoulou

State Theatre
of N. Greece

Megalou Alexandrou

White Tower
[Byzantine Museum]

Ethnological and
Popular Museum

Yachting Club

1. Tourist Office.
2. Archaeological Museum.
3. Aliens' Bureau.
4. Tourists Police - Traffic Police.
5. Central Post Office.
6. Town Hall.
7. Port Authority.
8. First Aid Station.
9. Olympic Airlines Ticket Agent.
10. Ladadika
11. New Byzantine Museum

Tips for beginners

When to go If you have to time your visit to fit in with school holidays or other constraints, you will obviously be going in late July or August. By doing so, you can at least be virtually certain of unbroken blue skies and high temperatures and that sea or pool water won't give you goose bumps. However, as in all other major resort areas, holidays in Halkidiki are more expensive at this time, although taverna, hotel and bar prices are legally controlled, so you won't get ripped off. However, everywhere will be much more crowded, especially at weekends when the numbers are swelled by Greek visitors. It's not just beaches, accommodation and eating and drinking places – the roads can turn into a chaotic scrum of hooting, manoeuvring cars clogging up the resorts and making parking a virtual impossibility. One useful tip to remember is that Greeks tend to eat relatively late. They'll rarely begin lunch before 1.30 p.m. or dinner before 10 p.m., so you can time your own meals to either enjoy some local colour or avoid the busiest time as your inclination takes you.

It's worth knowing too that the centres of some of the popular resorts can be quite noisy until the early hours. We're not talking lager louts or 18–30 style bars here – you are unlikely to see anyone wearing Union Jack shorts or singing 'Here we go' at 4 a.m. However, the Greeks themselves tend to stay up late, especially the young people, and many of the bars will stay open until the last customer leaves, so if you're staying close to the centre of a resort, be prepared for this in the high season.

The season starts around the end of April or the beginning of May, which is when charter flights start operating and most of the hotels open for business. In some respects, early May is one of the nicest times to go. The biggest attraction – apart from the lack of crowds – is the masses of wild flowers blooming absolutely everywhere you look. Fields and roadsides are a picture, with scarlet poppies and dozens of other varieties of yellow, white and purple flowers that are a real feast for the eyes. You'll even see flowers blooming amongst the pebbles or in the rough sand at the edge of beaches where you'd think nothing could possibly grow. While the weather should be pleasantly warm, and the sun often shines, you have to remember that you don't get all this luxurious growth without quite a bit of rain. Having twice been in Halkidiki at the beginning of May in consecutive years, I have to say that I saw more rain and clouds than sun both times, which would obviously be a major disappointment for would-be sunbathers. Another point worth noting is that, while most bars and tavernas are open, you'll probably find there's still quite a bit of repainting, sawing and hammering going on around the place as people get ready for the new season. Beach facilities too are often not quite in full swing – 'the windsurfers/pedaloes/sun umbrellas come next week' is a common refrain, and beach snack bars may not have opened yet. The same can be said of the nightlife – and there's nothing sadder than a discotheque pulling out all the stops for a dozen or so patrons sitting around the edges of the dance floor waiting in vain for the place to fill up.

By late June/early July, everything is in full swing, but the area is still not overcrowded. During the day, it can get seriously hot – over 40°C, and the humidity is high. Few people have the energy to do anything more than lie by pool or sea, preferably in the shade, making the odd excursion to bar or taverna for refreshment. The sea is like a warm bath, and it can still feel hot in the evenings if there isn't a breeze. These conditions produce thunderstorms, which as well as being refreshing and spectacular to watch, are an entertainment in themselves. The rain starts suddenly and comes down so heavily that within minutes the streets are turned into fast-flowing streams.

If you happen to be in a village, you can shelter under an awning and watch the ensuing panic. Umbrellas appear from nowhere, and everyone starts to rush around like characters in a speeded-up film, clearing away displays from in front of the shops and scurrying for cover. Cars splash through the instant puddles, with water half-way over their wheels, and there's a lot of shouting and laughing. Crowds gather in tavernas and bars or shelter in doorways, watching the lightning flash over the mountains or the sea, and then within 20 minutes or so, it's all over. It takes rather longer for the water to drain away, though, but there's a pleasant freshness to the air and the streets and pathways are clear of dust for a while. August is the season of highest temperatures and biggest crowds, and ideal if you like to go when everything is in full swing and buzzing with life.

For those who like things a little quieter, September is perfect. The sea is just the right temperature to cool you off without giving you a shock, while the skies are blue with usually a breeze to counter the heat of the sun. The main resorts, especially in Kassandra, are still full of holidaymakers, although you may find that some of the tavernas which are particularly popular with Greek customers start to close down as the month progresses. This is the time when the grapes ripen. You'll find shops almost giving them away, and you can sit under vine-covered awnings with great bunches of grapes weighing down their branches. Although the days are shorter, with the sun setting at about 7.30 p.m. by the middle of September, the evenings are still warm enough to sit around outside without a cardigan or jacket.

Weather	temperature °C	
	max	min
May	26	14.1
June	32	19
July	33	20.4
August	34	19.4
September	30	18.4
October	29	13.4

In practice, you're far more likely to encounter temperatures closer to the maximum figures, although it can feel quite cool when it rains early in the season.

The language Although hundreds of returning holidaymakers enrol for Greek language evening classes every September, few last longer than a term or two. The simple reason is that modern Greek is a difficult language to master, and it's not that easy even to pick up the basics. For most people, the alphabet is the major obstacle, at least initially, and capital and lower case versions of the same letter often look quite different. From a practical point of view, road signs, place names and other important notices are nearly always written in English as well as Greek. Road signs before junctions usually come in two versions: you'll see the Greek one first, then the English one a few yards further on, although occasionally both languages will be on the same sign. In the smaller places, street names and sometimes even taverna and bar signs will be in Greek only. Menus will come in English – although you may sometimes need a little imagination to understand what they actually mean.

You won't have any language problem in the hotels, and probably not in the resorts either because everyone will speak either good English or enough to get by without too much trouble. Nevertheless, the locals will be delighted if you can manage just a few words, even if it's just 'please', and 'thank you' or 'good morning'. Once you forget about the strange alphabet, the sound of Greek is not that difficult for English speakers, and you can have a lot of fun trying to hold a conversation with the aid of a basic phrasebook. Talking is a national pastime in Greece, but courtesy usually requires the stranger to make the first move to open the conversation. Before you know it, you can be exchanging information about where you come from, what you do, what you think of Greece and the Greeks and just about anything else. The Greeks are great travellers, and have often visited Britain as well as other countries or even worked abroad, and have plenty to say on the subject. You can add a whole new dimension to your holiday by making an effort to talk to the local people, especially if you're staying in one of the larger hotel complexes, where it can sometimes be hard to remember that you're actually in Greece.

If you don't put the emphasis in the right place in a Greek word, it may not be understood. In the list below, you stress the syllable in bold type.

useful words and phrases	*Pronunciation*
hello	**yass**oo
good morning	kalli-**mare**-a
good evening	kalli-**spare**-a
good night	kalli-**nik**ta
yes	nay
no	**o**-hey (the 'o' sounds like it does in 'dog')
please	para-ka-**low**
thank you	eff-ha-ris-**toe**
OK	en-**dax**i
cheers	**yam**-ass
let's go	**pa**-may
today	**si**-mare-a
tomorrow	**av**-rio

Numbers	
one	**en**na
two	**thee**-oe
three	**tree**-a
four	**tess**-ara
five	**pen**tay
six	**ex**i

seven	ep-**ta**
eight	ok**toe**
nine	enn-**ya**
ten	**the**ka

Days of the week

Monday	thev-**ter**ra
Tuesday	**tri**-ti
Wednesday	tet-**are**-ti
Thursday	**pemp**-ti
Friday	para-skev-**ee**
Saturday	**savv**-adoe
Sunday	kirri-ar-**ki**

Money

The unit of currency is the drachma, and in September 1994 the exchange rate was 366 to £1. This is considerably better than the rate a year or so previously, and helps to compensate for the fact that Greece is not as cheap to visit as it once was. The economy is struggling, and inflation is a continuing problem, so the exchange rate may continue to favour British tourists for some time to come. If you're planning any major shopping expeditions, it's worth having a solar-powered calculator with you to make sure you don't end up spending a fortune on what you thought was a bargain. Dividing thousands of drachmas by, say, 350 in your head isn't a simple matter for all of us, and it's all too easy to lose track of a crucial nought. You can exchange sterling travellers' cheques at your hotel, although they do sometimes run out of currency if there has been a run on their supplies. This is most likely on days when the banks are closed, which is, of course, just when you need them most. You will probably get a better exchange rate at a bank so it can be worth planning to change your money when they're open. Don't be fooled by the fact that many banks have security locks on their doors – if you push and pull without managing to open the door, it doesn't necessarily mean the bank is closed! Look for a buzzer to press and wait for the staff to release the door electronically. Sometimes, though, it's just a question of pushing hard on the door. Once inside, you usually have to go to one person to sign your cheques and you'll probably be asked for your passport too. Then you'll be given a chitty to take to the cashier – which may well mean queuing twice.

Tips for beginners

Bank opening times
Monday to Thursday and Saturday: 8.30 a.m. – 2 p.m.; Friday: 8.30 a.m. – 1.30 p.m. Even when you have thought ahead, you can sometimes be surprised because the bank is unexpectedly closed for a public holiday. There are 24-hour cash dispensers in the towns and a couple of larger resorts which will not only exchange British notes for Greek, but also allow you to withdraw money on Visa or Access cards, provided you know your PIN number. The screen has instructions in English on how to operate the machine, and also displays the exchange rate before you proceed. If you're not too bothered about losing the odd few drachmas in an exchange deal, you can change currency and travellers' cheques in bureaux de change and travel agents, many of which stay open until 9 or 10 p.m. and on Saturdays and Sundays. You won't find a proper post office in all resorts, but if there does happen to be one near you, it's useful to know that they'll cash travellers' cheques and Eurocheques, provided you have a card and your passport with you, and will also change currency. Otherwise you'll need to look for a bank displaying the EC symbol, or cash them at a bureau de change.

Credit cards
It's worth taking your card with you, especially if you plan to do any major shopping. Shops and some restaurants in Thessaloniki mostly accept the major cards, and you'll be able to pay your hotel extras bill with one too if you want to. However, with a few exceptions, local restaurants and tavernas are unlikely to accept them, so if you want to pay with plastic, check before you eat! Similarly, some tourist shops are happy to take a credit card, but in most you'll need cash.

Local geography
There are a variety of maps available from souvenir shops, newsagents and elsewhere, some more useful and easier to read than others. The one supplied by Hertz has a handy map of Thessaloniki on the back, although the small one available from the tourist office is easier to use. For general navigation, I found the road map produced by the German publishers Freytag and Berndt the most practical, and its map of Thessaloniki is much more detailed than either of the others, although a bit unwieldy when you're on foot.

One real difficulty is that, while maps give street names in both Greek and English, signs on the roads themselves often don't. In Thessaloniki, you'll find all the major and some of the minor roads labelled in English, but this is rare elsewhere. In any case, there are no maps which include street plans of any of the resorts, which is why my directions veer towards the descriptive rather than the precise. As it wouldn't take more than an hour to walk round the largest resort, this isn't generally a major problem, however. No one is in a hurry on holiday, and wandering about exploring is half the fun. While many shops and bars have signs in English, the same isn't always true of tavernas. Some names you can guess from the Greek signs – Nikos looks quite similar, for example, in either language, but most you can't. So, once again, information about how to find them is frequently of the 'white building with blue shutters and red awning next to the jetty' variety.

Transport

Buses. Greek buses are an institution. They may look somewhat beaten up and appear to move according to strange unwritten laws, but once you get the hang of them, they are a cheap and reliable way of getting around. From the tourists' point of view, the main difficulty is that their routes and timetables are – naturally enough – based on the requirements of the local people, which may not always accord with yours. This means that they tend to be more frequent in the early morning and early evening, and rather sparse during the day. It also means that while it is perfectly simple to get a bus from, say Kallithea in Kassandra to Thessaloniki, it is more difficult to get one to the neighbouring peninsula of Sithonia (you have to change at Nea Moudania) and impossible to get one to Athos without going via Thessaloniki.

They are ideal, though, if you simply want to see other places on the peninsula where you're staying, and for getting to and from Thessaloniki. Because they serve inland villages as well as the coastal resorts, the buses give you the opportunity to see something of the countryside and rural life on your journey. Fares are reasonable, and you buy your ticket from the driver, except at the bus station in Thessaloniki where there is a ticket office. Timetables are often stuck up in travel agents' windows, sometimes chalked on notice boards by the terminus and should also be available from your hotel reception or tour operator's representative. There are stops in all the villages, outside some of the major hotels and at many beaches – usually with a small shelter and a few seats. Queuing is rudimentary, but it's rare for anyone to get left behind – which can lead to a certain amount of overcrowding at popular times!

Amazingly in a country where virtually everyone seems

to smoke, it is not permitted on buses – except sometimes by the drivers. Windows have curtains to draw against the sun, some buses have a rather ineffective form of air conditioning and you will frequently be treated to constant Greek music from the driver's radio.

Bus timetables – see page 129.

Car hire. This tends to be expensive, and you will usually get a better rate by booking a car through your tour operator at the same time as you book your holiday. You could expect to save as much as 10,000 drachmas for a three-day booking on the basic models, such as a Seat Marbella. Otherwise, it's easy enough to make arrangements once you're in the resort. Your tour operator's rep can arrange it for you, or you can simply go to or phone one of the hire companies yourself. Alternatively, most of the exchange bureaux-cum-travel agents can make the necessary arrangements and you can either pick up the car there or have it delivered to your hotel. You have to be at least 21, and to have held a driving licence for 12 months – they'll want to see it.

The main hire companies have offices in Thessaloniki (T) and Kallithea (K):

Avis – 031 227 126 (T); 0374 23 320/23 349 (K).
Hertz – 031 224 906 (T); 0374 22 960/22 969 (K).
Interrent/Europcar – 031 826 333 (T); 0374 23 309 (K).
Atlas – 031 325 845 (T); 0374 237 501 (K).

There's not a lot to choose as far as prices are concerned, although in 1994 Hertz was marginally the cheapest. For a basic car such as a Seat Marbella, prices range from 3,700 per day (plus mileage) to 43,080 for three days (unlimited mileage) in the low season, to 4,600 daily and 53,460 for three days in the high season. These prices include only the basic legal minimum of insurance cover. Theft protection, collision damage waiver and personal accident insurance can all be bought as extras, and are worthwhile, if only for peace of mind. You will not have the equivalent of fully comprehensive insurance unless you buy both the extras mentioned. There is also 18 per cent tax payable on top, and petrol at around 200 drachmas per litre is extra.

Driving. With the exception of Thessaloniki, driving is easy and enjoyable. The main roads are good and well-surfaced, although those marked in yellow on maps are usually unmade but still navigable at low speed. In high season, especially at weekends, the roads do get very clogged, and there are actually traffic jams in the main resorts like Kallithea and Neos Marmaras. Central Thessaloniki is a permanent jam, but perfectly manageable to anyone used to driving in big cities in this country. Don't worry if you get hooted at – it's normal practice and isn't likely to mean you've done anything particularly dreadful or dangerous. Despite the tendency to hoot at the slightest (or even nil) provocation, Greek drivers are amazingly tolerant of dithering foreigners, easily identifiable by their hire cars emblazoned with company logos.

Apart from in the city, there are few traffic lights, although you do come across them occasionally at major junctions or at the approaches to some villages. A flashing amber light is a warning of lights ahead or sometimes of traffic turning into your path from a side road; otherwise traffic lights turn from red to green without any amber. You do get an amber, however, when they're going from green to red! A few major roads are dual carriageway, and others have a hard shoulder to which you are expected to retreat to allow overtaking. You will be overtaken by everything except the odd agricultural vehicle. Most drivers take no notice of speed limits, and little of double lines in the middle of the road. Speed limits vary depending on the type of road, and you will find them on the approaches to villages and junctions, where you should slow down. It's advisable to take notice of this, even if no one else does, because there are frequently tourists wandering in the road or looking the wrong way before they cross. You are supposed to wear seat belts outside towns and villages, though few do, and the drink driving laws are honoured more in the breach . . .

Again with the exception of Thessaloniki and some of the larger resorts, parking is unrestricted, and in practice most people tend to stop and abandon their cars in the most unlikely places, usually without signalling. Theoretically, you can't park right in the centre of Thessaloniki, and although people do, it's not to be recommended. For more about parking in Thessaloniki, see page 45.

There is the odd regulation that may flummox you. For example, in Neos Marmaras, a road which I had driven up quite happily (and legally) one day turned into a one-way street overnight. The policeman enforcing the new rule was giving out tickets to all miscreants, but after staring at me very fiercely and demanding to know where I came from, simply told me to go, indicating that I should turn the car round back in the direction I had come from. The new system had been introduced that day and applied just for July and August, and apparently foreigners ignorant of the rules were allowed a certain leeway not permitted to locals.

When you park, try to imitate the local people whenever possible and choose a shady spot. If you don't the car will be like a sauna when you return, and the steering wheel and gear lever too hot to touch. In many villages, locking your car and closing the windows every time you leave it, and always wearing your seat belt are regarded as amusingly eccentric, but it is still better to be safe than sorry, however small the risk.

Petrol stations are everywhere and usually signposted ahead, and many of them stay open into the early hours. It's a pleasant novelty to find that they are rarely self-service, and the helpful staff will often offer to pump up your tyres as well if they think it necessary. They'll normally assume you want the tank filled, but if you want to ask, the phrase is 'Yem**ees**tay to ('o' as in dog) para-kal**loe**'. Remember to check when you collect the car what kind of petrol it takes. Unleaded is available everywhere, but models which can use it in the UK cannot necessarily do so in Greece. The Fiat Panda I drove in Halkidiki ran on super, unlike the one I have here which takes unleaded petrol.

Taxis. When you want to travel a relatively short distance – say from your hotel to the next village or back at night from a taverna or bar – a taxi is definitely the best option. They are very much cheaper than in the UK – a 10 to 15-minute journey is likely to cost around 1,000 drachmas after midnight, for example. Most resorts have a rank of sorts – even though there may be only a few taxis available, and you will often find them waiting for customers outside the big hotels. Alternatively, your hotel reception will call one for you, as will many tavernas and bars. Hailing one as it passes in the street is not normal practice, except in Thessaloniki. Then it is worth trying, even if the yellow light on the roof is on, indicating that it's already occupied. If you happen to be going the same way as the incumbent passenger, you'll be invited to share the cab, each of you paying separately for your own journey.

Bicycles. For getting around your resort and small-scale expeditions, bikes are the perfect choice. They're available for hire at the larger hotels and in many resorts, usually for around 1,500 drachmas a day. Mostly they're mountain bikes, which is handy as the roads tend towards the hilly, and especially useful if you want to venture inland. Many

The traditional craft of boat building is still flourishing.

of the same outfits also rent mopeds and motor bikes. Although cheaper than a car and requiring less effort than a pushbike, they can be hazardous for the unwary, and most tour operators will probably warn you against them. Every year, hundreds of tourists have accidents, which range in seriousness from severe grazing, cuts and bruises to broken limbs and worse. If you do decide to go ahead, check the insurance cover carefully, wear a crash helmet and don't ride wearing nothing but a swimming costume or shorts and a T-shirt. Apart from the real risk of sunburn, you'll have no protection at all if you do come off, and the damage to your skin will be much worse.

Boats. Ports and harbours around Halkidiki aren't full of the constant comings and goings of ferry boats you see in most other parts of Greece. While you can go by Flying

Dolphin from Nea Moudania, Marmaras and Pefkohori to the north Aegean islands of Skiathos, Skopelos, Alonisos and Skyros, most boat trips go no further than nearby beaches. There is a regular car ferry from Tripiti at the top of Athos to the nearby island of Amouliani (see page 25). You can also go on the boat trip along the coast of Athos to see some of the famous monasteries – excursions run from several ports in Sithonia and from Kassandra.

If you have the cash to spare, hiring a small motor boat for the day is a lovely way to explore the hidden coves along the various coastlines. Prices are around 7–8,000 drachmas a day plus petrol – look for 'Boat rent' signs in all the big resorts and on some of the hotel beaches.

Sport

Watersports – or more often, water fun and games – are easily the most popular, especially in high summer when it's too hot to contemplate any other activity. Facilities are confined in general to the beaches attached to the bigger hotels – although you don't have to be a guest to use them. Windsurfing is not as prevalent here as elsewhere in Greece, but when it is available, equipment is likely to be of a high standard, with lessons available for beginners. The same is true of water-skiing, but most people seem to opt for activities that require less skill and dedication to perfect. Jet-skis – noisy little things like water-borne motor bikes – are increasingly popular, as is the so-called 'banana'. This is an inflated yellow contraption which several people sit astride, one behind the other, to be towed along, with the driver doing his best to tip you into the water every time he turns the boat. You may also find parascending – dangling from a parachute over the water as you're towed along by the boat below – plus the usual pedaloes and canoes for hire. In one or two places, there are scuba diving centres, with lessons from qualified instructors, notably at the excellent centre in Porto Carras. Water polo, aquarobics and other pool games are organised by the 'animation teams' in many of the hotels – you'll find details on their noticeboards.

Golf. At Porto Carras, there's an 18-hole golf course. You see it on your right as you come down into the resort and there's a sign a bit further on directing you to the club where you can get more information. There's a riding stables and school nearby too, also signposted, and you can also ride at Kriopigi and Hanioti in Kassandra.

Tennis. Many of the big hotels have tennis courts to rent by the hour for a few thousand drachmas, and sometimes equipment as well. In general, you'll find hard courts, although there are one or two with artificial turf and those at the Sani Beach Hotel and Club have a special shock-absorbant quartz sand surface. Most people prefer to play early in the day or later on when it's cooler, so you'd be well advised to book in advance at reception rather than just turn up on spec. Most of the courts are floodlit after dark, which is often the best time of day to play.

Walking

Outside July and August, this is perfect walking country. The scenery is stunning and you can walk for miles along shady paths without seeing a single soul. Some of the paths are steep and relatively rough, so if you plan more than a gentle stroll, take some sturdy walking shoes with you. You may not come across too many bars or tavernas, depending on where you walk and the time of year, so it's wise to take a good supply of water or other drinks with you. It's all too easy to get dehydrated without realising it. Mostly, you can walk under the shade of the woods, but it's sensible to have a sunhat for extra protection too.

In spring, when the wild flowers are out, it is a true feast for the eyes and so beautiful it's hard to believe it's real. Later in the season, the flowers are not so prolific, but there always seems to be something in bloom, and the woods are lovely all year round.

The resorts on Kassandra are rarely more than a few kilometres apart, and you can often walk along the beach or through the woodland behind from one to the other, but the mountains make this more difficult in Sithonia. If you want to try something more than a short local stroll, there is an excellent series of walks planned and signposted by the Halkidiki Hotel Association. All pass through lovely country, usually with views of the coastline, and they are clearly marked with red circles on boards at intervals along the way. The Association has produced a very good guide booklet giving full details, but I've summarised the crucial information below. At the time of writing, the booklet is only available in German, but there are plans to bring out an English edition before long.

Kassandra
1 Fourka to Kassandria
Start: Hotel Avra, Fourka; time: two and a half hours. Where the road ends at the Avra Hotel, a sandy path climbs up quite steeply, bending to the right and

continuing up through the cornfields and pine woods. As the path levels out, you get a view of Fourka and the sea down below. A few metres on, the path curves round to the left, and when it divides, you take the left fork. Now you continue along the main path, following the signs to the centre of Kassandria, where you'll see the cathedral and the old windmills. From here, you can get a taxi or a bus back to your starting point.

2 Sani Beach circuit
Start: Hotel Sani Beach; time: two and a half hours.
You turn right (north) along the road at the hotel complex exit, which follows the edge of the woods. There's an open field in front of you and you keep going until you come to a tower-like building which is a pumping station. It's used to clear the water which covers this area early in the year. In spring and early autumn, it's something of a sanctuary for resident and migratory birds, so don't forget your binoculars. Turn sharp left (west) by the pumping station, and follow the path through the pines down to the beach. You can have a rest and a drink in the bar overlooking the marina. Alternatively, you can do a longer version by following the path round to the right at the pumping station, then returning along the beach.

3 Kriopigi mountain circuit
Start: Kriopigi; time: around five hours.
Follow the side street up from the coastal road to the inland village of Kriopigi, passing the church and police station on your left. Keep going west until you come to a fork and take the road signposted to Kassandria – it's in Greek, but most of the letters are the same. The road winds through woods then cornfields, and just before you get to Kassandrino, go straight over the crossroads until you reach the made up road, where you turn left and carry on into the village. Here you can have a break and a drink, then you continue out through the other side of the village and keep on the same path until you come to a fork. Take a rough path that climbs up steeply to the left with a fantastic view from the top. Your route then goes back down, and you keep to the left until you eventually come to the Kassandrino–Kriopigi road. Bear left and continue till you come to a little field track on your right. It takes you past a fountain and through bushes back to the church of Kriopigi.

4 Agia Paraskevi to Kassandrino and Fourka
Start: Agia Paraskevi; time: four to five hours.

Halkidiki

There's a bus that will take you to Agia Paraskevi from Kallithea and the resorts to the north or from Siviri, Fourka and Nea Skioni, or you can take a taxi. The start is on the upper road which leads to Kassandrino and the path goes through pine woods with glimpses of the sea. You'll notice little plastic bags hung from the trees to catch the resin (used for retsina and also in pharmacy) and hundreds of colourful beehives. Eventually you come to a crossroads where the sign directs you down to the right. The path drops steeply down into Kassandrino, where you'll find a couple of tavernas, and if it's a Sunday or a holiday, you should find lamb being spit-roasted in the one on the right. From Kassandrino, the route goes to Kriopigi, Kassandria and Skala Fourkas – where you can cool off with a swim.

Sithonia

1 Neos Marmaras to Parthenonas
Start: Taverna Drosia (on coast road 1 km north of Marmaras); time: two hours.

The dusty track winds uphill for 5 km through olive groves with wonderful views over the countryside. You'll probably be passed by the odd car or tractor and a few motor bikes, and you keep going until you reach Paul's taverna at the top of the village. For more about this and Parthenonas itself, see page 105. If you want to take a different way down ask Paul to show you where the path starts and it will bring you back down on to the main road, 100 m from the track to Neos Marmaras.

2 Nikiti to Ormos Panagias
Start: Nikiti old town; time: four hours.

Heading east from the old town, past the cathedral and graveyard, you get on to a steep stony path, and there's a little church up above which you can detour to visit – but it's very steep! You continue on the main path through pine woods, going up all the time. When the path forks, go right to the summit, then take the path to the right (south) through a thick pine forest. You'll see the church of Agios Giorgios, and below, lagoons, beaches and Diaporas island, with Athos in the distance. Eventually, the path takes you to the village of Agios Nikolaos where you can rest and have a drink. Onwards to the south-east, taking the left of two parallel roads. About 100 m before the end of the town, bear left going north-east on a tarmac road. After a sign listing lots of places including Salouniou beach, keep going, past another sign in Greek, for 2 km until you reach the sea. Ormos Panagias is a pretty little

Tips for beginners

Herdsmen tending their sheep are a common sight all over Halkidiki.

fishing village with a small harbour and a few tavernas, and at the end of the beach you'll see the bus stop for your return journey.

3 Neos Marmaras to Porto Carras
Start: Neos Marmaras; time: around five hours.
Walk along the beach to the Porto Carras complex which you can see along the coast to the marina, and on through the hotel area to the golf course. The path runs parallel to the main road up 500 m to the Cava Carras. There are tours and wine-tastings every day except Sunday and Tuesday from 8 a.m.–12 p.m. and 1 p.m.–3 p.m. Just beyond the Cava, you swing right on to an unmade road and continue until you come to a sign saying Europa Beach 6 km. Directly above, you can see the Carras family home

perched on the mountain. There's a campsite at Europa beach where you can have a drink. It's said there are thirty-five bays between there and Porto Carras – so you can find one all to yourself for a swim. After about 5 km, you come to the barrier in the road which is where the hotel bus ends its journey, and from there you're soon back in Porto Carras itself.

4 Sykia to the hidden coves
Start: Sykia; time: around two hours.
You can get to the pretty inland village of Sikia (see page 111) by bus from either coast of Sithonia. The path starts behind the highest village houses and takes you towards the summit. You'll be better off with trousers than shorts because the path is rocky and overhung with bushes. The path leads south and becomes easier, turning east towards the sea. You'll see Mount Athos in front of you all the way, and keep an eye open for the red dot markers to get you through some gardens and over a field to the road. When you meet it, turn right until you can join the sandy path running alongside. After about 500 m, turn left down to Skala Sykias, where you can have a swim, or continue east to find the dozen tiny hidden bays. The bus stop for your return journey is in Skala Sykias.

5 The mountains of Petros and Pavlos
Start: Hotel Lagomandra (around 5 km north of Neos Marmaras); time: around four hours.
About 100 m south of the hotel, opposite the Lagomandra beach sign, take a stony track uphill and fork left through the olive grove when the path widens. In about an hour you'll see Mount Petros ahead of you through the pines, and the path leads on through the woods. Be warned – the climb up is hard going and you need stout shoes, but the view when you arrive is worth it as you see the whole of the east coast spread before you. Next you cross an open fire-break area, and at the crossroads, there's a sign pointing downwards to Agios Pavlos. Below you'll see the tiny church where the Apostle Paul on his way to Corinth is said to have struck a rock with his stick and created the spring beside the church. At weekends, the area is crowded with people coming to fill containers and bottles with the spring water. The path restarts above the church by the hostel and heads southwest through the valley. You cross the main coast road onto a path down to a beautiful beach. After your swim, turn left off the beach by the painted sign pointing to Agios Nikolaos and in 2 km the path will take you to the main road and the bus stop.

6 Hotel Azapiko to Toroni.
Start: Hotel Azapiko, on the main road between Neos Marmaras and Toroni; time: four to five hours.
The bus stops about 1 km from the hotel, and you walk south past the campsite fence and the next headland, to reach two quiet bays. At the end of the beach, the path goes up to a house then swings left and inland, and eventually reaches the campsite at Tristinika where you can get a drink at a kiosk. South from the campsite, you go through a gateway following the winding path up to the next headland. After another little beach, you come to the small resort of Toroni, about 15 minutes further on. From there, it's steeply uphill over the peak to the lovely fishing harbour of Porto Koufo (see page 110).

Athos

1 A peep at the Holy Mountain
Start: Ouranoupolis; time: one hour.
Walk through Ouranoupolis (the Town of Heaven) with the sea on your right, and up the hill at the end. The road turns into a track, and you keep on along it for about half an hour, until you see the ruins of a thousand-year-old castle on your left, almost hidden by the trees. Just a few paces beyond you come to the border of the monastic republic – the nearest you can get to setting foot inside! Then it's back to Ouranoupolis for a swim or a boat trip along the coast to see some of the monasteries (see page 126).

2 Around Amouliani
Start: Tripiti (for the ferry to the island); time: three hours.
After the 20-minute boat trip to the island of Amouliani, formerly a kind of penal colony for errant monks (see page 119), at the Mega Market just on the edge of the village, you turn right along a field path, leading past a dried up salt pit. In half an hour, you come to a long beach by the campsite, with a taverna at one end. At the other end, there's a narrow field path which you can take if you have time for a bit more exploring. Depending on which boat you're getting back to the mainland, you can have a drink or a wander around the village.

3 From gulf to gulf
Start: Ouranoupolis; time: four hours.
At the edge of the village you'll find a road that winds up to a chapel in the trees, then heads overland towards the opposite coast. There are many lovely beaches on the way to Ierissos, but one of the most beautiful is Koumitsa, on

the other side of the peninsula, with lovely views of the Holy Mountain.

4 Ouranoupolis to Nea Roda
Start: Ouranoupolis; time: around five hours.
On the road out of Ouranoupolis, near the Alexandros and Eagles Palace Hotels, there's a narrow path leading up to a wide plateau. From there, you take a broad track running parallel with the road that goes straight to Nea Roda, and overlooks the plain where in 480 BC, the Persian commander Xerxes cut a canal to save his ships the dangerous voyage around the tip of Athos (see page 37). Here you can either go for a swim at Koumitsa (see Walk 3) or continue eastwards along the parallel inland road. You return to Ouranoupolis by the unmade road.

5 Arnea
Start: Arnea; time: three hours.
You can get a bus or taxi from Athos to Arnea, or if you have a car, make a brief stop in the village of Stagira to see the statue of the philosopher Aristotle, who, say the villagers, was born there. In Arnea (see page 42), go left past the town hall and left again. You go along the unmade road past the church and children's playground, until you come to a track on the right. This winds slowly up the 'Saints'' hill to the little church of Elijah. From this vantage point, you have a good view of Arnea itself and the surrounding farmland.

Food and drink

When it comes to eating and drinking, there's plenty of choice. Eateries come in many forms: tavernas including specialist fish ones called psarotavernas, restaurants (estiatoria), ouzeria, snack bars and pizzerias, although the distinctions are not always very clear. Even so-called pizzerias often offer quite a wide-ranging choice of other dishes as well, although the majority of snack bars tend towards the fast-food options and are usually less interesting. There are also cafés and bars which may have some food, plus the zacharoplasteia which are a great institution. Some are simply cake and pastry shops, while others also have tables where you can sample their wares with a coffee or cold drink or sometimes an ice cream. It's OK almost anywhere to have just a drink rather than a meal – although some tavernas and restaurants like you to sit at the unlaid tables if you're not eating. Greek ice cream isn't quite on a par with Italian, but it's much better than most of ours. Ice cream parlours abound in the resorts, and usually offer a baffling range of choices, including some which are served in sundae glasses and come with all sorts of exciting sauces.

Menus can be difficult to interpret – for one thing, translations from the Greek are not always enlightening. You'll often find that you're given a standard printed menu – the dishes with prices written in against them will usually be available, although not always. Sometimes you may be told that certain dishes are only on offer in July and August – that is, when the Greek holidaymakers come, but this doesn't happen all that often. Alternatively, you could be invited into the kitchen to choose from what you can see – often there are prepared dishes as well as uncooked ingredients (especially fish) for your inspection. I always find I order more in this situation because I can't bear to miss out.

Many people are surprised to discover that there's a lot more to Greek food than moussaka, kebabs and taramosalata – although you'll find all these on most menus. You won't find many complicated dishes or fancy sauces. Rather the approach is to take good, locally produced ingredients and cook them simply, often with the addition of fresh herbs. Meat lovers should find the lamb and chicken particularly good, and there's beef (or biftecki) on offer in most tavernas, although sometimes it may be veal rather than beef as we know it. Souvlakia (kebabs) with the meat or chicken (or sometimes fish, especially swordfish) sometimes interspersed with onion, tomato and peppers are usually cooked on a charcoal grill and served with rice. Another good bet are the various casserole-style dishes, such as stifado. These require long slow cooking, often in a clay pot, with potatoes or onions and herbs added to the meat.

One of the local specialities is tripe. You'll see it on menus as kokkinisto – which is usually kebabs of liver and tripe. I am sorry to have to confess that I haven't tried it, but those with a stronger stomach might like to give it a whirl.

Fresh fish and seafood is one of the delights of Halkidiki. Exactly what's on the menu will depend to some extent on the season and the day's catch. Some of the fish don't have English names, so the best thing is to ask what they are, and often you'll be taken to the kitchen to see for yourself. Of the more familiar varieties, cod fried in a light batter (vakalaos) is delicious, especially when served with skordalia – a piquant, if somewhat anti-social kind of garlic-based bread sauce. Mussels are popular too. You'll come across them in tomato sauce, grilled or fried, or as a local speciality, in a kind of risotto.

The fish prices on the menu may look alarming because they are quoted by the kilo, and individual portions are much more reasonable. Even so, anything other than the small varieties such as gopes or millini is likely to be more expensive than many of the other items on the menu. It is worth going for it at least once, though, because it really is wonderful.

For a more economical feast, choose a selection of starters and side dishes which make up 'mezedes'. Among my favourites are stuffed aubergine, white beans in onion and tomato sauce, fried sweet red or green peppers, cheese saganaki – triangles of cheese coated in flour and fried, dolmadakia – baby stuffed vine leaves, taramosalata, tzatziki and Greek salad topped with feta cheese. Most tavernas in Halkidiki have two kinds of salad which you don't often see elsewhere in Greece – sweet red peppers and beetroot cooked with its leaves – which are definitely worth trying. As well as the stuffed aubergine known as imam, (filled with a tomato and onion mixture), you'll see a local version filled with feta and sweet red pepper which is very good. You'll also come across htipiti – feta cheese with whole green peppercorns. It has a consistency something like scrambled egg but with a real bite. Many menus feature salted fish – especially anchovies – among their starters, or fresh sardines, tuna or anchovies in oil.

For two of you, around six or seven dishes would be about right. Greeks usually go for a mixture of salads, fish, something a bit more filling – like stuffed aubergine or beans, tzatziki and perhaps something hot, like village sausages or fried cheese. Traditionally, you should have them with ouzo, but retsina goes very well with them too.

Otherwise, as in the rest of Greece, it's not much use thinking in terms of starters followed by a main course. Your bread and drinks will be brought immediately, but after that the food will arrive in whatever order it is ready. So you're very likely to get, say salad, cold starters and chips first, with other hot dishes coming along a bit later. You soon get used to this, and the bonus is that nearly everything is prepared and cooked when you order it, rather than sitting around for hours in advance.

Apart from chips (patates), you won't find much in the way of vegetables as accompaniments. Greeks tend to opt for vegetable-based side dishes and salads instead, and puddings are a definite rarity in tavernas. It's worth remembering that many dishes which the Greeks call salads are actually more like dips. The main ones, apart from taramosalata, are aubergine salad, Russian salad and tzatziki, which is sometimes described as cucumber and yoghurt salad.

Don't forget that if you're unsure what to order, the waiters will usually be more than willing to advise and help you choose something you'll enjoy. I have met British holidaymakers who say they stick to things they know because they don't want to make fools of themselves – which is sad because it means missing out on so many delicious tastes and a lot of fun.

Anyone who fancies something sweet and a coffee to finish a meal is more likely to move on to a zacharoplasteio – a cake and coffee place – or an ice cream parlour. Cakes and pastries, whether to finish a meal or as a daytime snack, are a real treat. Many are based on the flaky filo pastry and involve the liberal addition of nuts, especially walnuts, and honey, but there are many other varieties. One of the nicest are the tiny light doughnut-style concoctions dripping in honey, called loukoumades. Usually, you can go up to the counter and point or ask what's what, and the choice is usually larger in the daytime than in the evening. One Halkidiki speciality you shouldn't miss is bugatsa. It's made of filo and filled with either cheese or a confectioner's cream topped with cinnamon and icing sugar. It's normally served warm (although it may only be available cold in the evening) and chopped into bite-sized pieces. Do try it.

Greek coffee is strong and black and comes in tiny cups with a thick residue in the bottom. If you like it, remember to specify whether you want it with sugar (metrio), very sweet (glyko) or without sugar (sketto). Otherwise, you can order what's universally known as Nescafé. Again you need to specify the sugar content in advance, and say if you want milk – which will be the evaporated variety from a tin. You can also have Nescafé in the same combinations as frappe (iced coffee) which is an ideal mid-morning drink on a hot day. Usually, you'll be served a glass of iced water along with your coffee, whether it's hot or cold.

Many people prefer to stick to soft drinks, mineral water or beer with meals. Occasionally you'll find draught beer – of the light, fizzy variety, but mostly it comes in half-litre bottles, with Amstel, Heineken and Lowenbrau the most common varieties. A large bottle of Amstel costs around 400 drachmas, and reasonable wine anything from around 1,100 drachmas. Much of the wine is ordinary or occasionally worse, but Halkidiki is a wine-producing area and there is also some very good stuff. The best by general consent is that grown and made by Château Carras – the world-famous vineyard and winery in Sithonia (see page 106). You'll also see several wines under the Boutari and Tsantali labels – much of which is produced in northern Greece and perfectly acceptable. Anything calling itself Makedoniko is local and usually quite all right, but those with delicate palates might want to steer clear of house wines, which are often listed on menus as 'wine from the barrel'. Retsina is on most lists too – and you either love or hate its resiny taste. If you've never tried it, don't give up after the first sip as the taste can take a bit of acquiring.

Ouzo and Greek brandy are, of course, widely available, but you'll also see a lot of local people drinking a clear spirit called tsipouro which is served in small glass jugs or sometimes in little bottles, often unlabelled. It is a local drink from the same family as Cretan raki, but with a less fiery taste and a pleasant flavour. It's often taken with the dishes of appetisers called mezedes, as an alternative to ouzo, or sometimes with fish dishes.

Beaches

Its 500 km coastline means Halkidiki can offer an unrivalled selection of beautiful beaches, ranging from shingle to fine sand. Outside the main resorts, they're frequently uncrowded, although in high summer any that are reasonably accessible will sport Greek families in small groups scattered around. Most will have some sort of beach bar where you can get a drink and maybe a simple snack, but the best bet is to take your own supplies as the locals do. Sunbeds, parasols, and watersports are generally confined to the main hotel beaches and a few in the bigger resorts, which can get pretty crowded. If you want to do most of your sunbathing and swimming away from the main hotel beaches, it is worthwhile investing in one of the sun umbrellas which are available in all the beach shops for around 3,000 drachmas. They're not too heavy to carry, and you just shove the end into the sand to provide instant shade. It's not always provided naturally, and you really do need to get out of the sun for at least part of the day.

Almost anywhere you choose to swim in Halkidiki, one thing you're guaranteed is clean, clear, unpolluted water and beaches. For 1994/5, the region's beaches have been awarded an astonishing 32 Blue Flags – the EC's coveted symbol of cleanliness. This is more than any other single region or prefecture in the country, and is an indication of both the unspoiled nature of the area, and the care taken by local people to make sure it stays that way.

Tips for beginners

You can walk for miles along the beautiful coastline without seeing another tourist.

Blue Flag beaches
Some resorts have several beaches, each of which has their own flag, but the resorts covered are:
Kassandra – Afitos, Kriopigi, Polihrono, Hanioti, Pefkhohori, Fourka, Possidi and Sani.
Sithonia – Sarti, Kalamitsi, Porto Carras, Neos Marmaras, Nikiti, Pyrgadikia, Metamorphosi, Psakoudia and Gerakini
Athos – Ouranoupolis, Olympiada.

Festivals   Apart from the Easter celebrations which go on everywhere, there are many local religious festivals throughout the year in the villages of Halkidiki. They are frequently associated with a particular saint, and take different forms depending on the place. Belief and religious observance are not confined to the elderly or to rural people as in many other European countries. Religion is a powerful force in Greece, and in fact belonging to the Greek Orthodox church is a part of their national identity for many people. A large proportion of the families in the area only moved there from Asia Minor in the 1921 exchange of populations with Turkey (see page 31). They brought with them the customs and traditions of their old lives, and memories of these are incorporated into the religious celebrations held every year.

Easter. The date varies, but it is always at least a week later than British Easter, so in some years it takes place after the holiday season has begun. Many people fast completely during Good Friday, and in the preceding days eat no meat or dairy foods. Through the three days of Easter, beginning on Good Friday, the faithful re-enact the death, burial and resurrection of Christ. Go into any of the churches on Good Friday, and you will see long lines of people waiting to kiss the 'pall', a piece of embroidered gold cloth, covered in fresh spring flowers, called the 'epitaphios', which symbolises the dead body of Christ. At nightfall, the epitaphios is carried in procession behind the Cross out of the church and around the streets. In Thessaloniki this is a terrific event, with bands preceding long processions from each of several churches through streets lined with people. All carry special yellow funeral candles, and many people follow the priests in the procession back to the church. Although it's a solemn occasion, the light of the thousands of flickering candles, the music and the crowds make it a fantastic spectacle and well worth seeing if you happen to be in the country at the right time.

On the Saturday, the atmosphere lightens, and in the evening there's a special service with white candles instead of yellow, and everyone dressed in their best clothes. At one point in the service, the few lights are extinguished to symbolise the darkness of the grave. Then, the priest appears at the door of the church holding a lighted candle, and announces to the waiting crowds that Christ is risen from the grave. All the candles are then lit, one from another, starting from the priest's, and he mounts a special scaffold for readings. At the end, the church bells ring, everyone waves their candles and exchange the 'kiss of the Resurrection'. At this moment the cacophony is tremendous – the sound of church bells is joined by guns and fireworks being let off and ships sound their sirens.

You are supposed to keep your candle alight until you get home – and in homes where there is an icon stand, the flame is used to renew the small light burning beneath it.

Then comes the special dinner, eaten late in the evening, with various traditional dishes. As well as hard-boiled eggs in their red-stained shells, you're likely to be offered a special soup called magiritsa. It has a distinctive taste, not improved by the knowledge that it's made from boiled lamb's intestines with dill and rice. Fortified by a few glasses of red wine beforehand, I found it quite palatable, but it's not everyone's favourite variety.

The traditional Easter Sunday meal is much more inviting – lamb roasted on a spit and basted with olive oil, oregano and lemon. You see them being cooked this way in gardens, outside tavernas and in village squares, and passers-by will be offered a taste and a glass of wine once it is ready.

Other festivals. Of the other festivals, one of the most interesting is at Neos Marmaras, the resort on the east coast of Sithonia. It begins at Pentecost, which is always 50 days after the Greek Easter, which means in May or June. Although the celebration has an important religious component, with the service of Vespers on the Saturday evening, it also reflects the traditions of the families' lives in their village in Asia Minor before 1920. On the Sunday evening, there is a representation of a traditional wedding in Asia Minor, then on the Monday, a re-enactment of the 'griphos' when the fishing boats go out into the bay and re-enact the way the community used to fish. Everyone wears traditional costume, and there's plenty of singing and dancing. If you are in Halkidiki at the right time – which will have to be worked out afresh each year from the date of Easter – it would be worth making the effort to see at least some of the celebrations.

Sani festival
Between June and September each year, there is a series of cultural events at the Sani Beach Holiday Resort in Kassandra. It includes concerts by well-known Greek and foreign artistes, dance performances, art exhibitions and 'Jazz on the hill' – the international three-day jazz festival. For lovers of classical music, there's Sani Classic, the two-week international classical music festival.

Some of the other main festivals in individual towns and villages are:

Ormilia – 30 June.
Nea Moudania Sardine Festival – July
Arnea – 26 July.
Parthenonas – 27 July.
Polygiros – 15 August.
Agios Mamas – 1 September (for three days).
Agios Nikolaos – 8 September.
Nea Roda and Nea Moudania – 8 September.

Other public holidays. Banks, post offices and many shops will be closed on the following dates:
New Year's Day – January 1.
Epiphany – January 6.
First Monday of Lent – moveable, depending on the date of Easter.

Traditional dancing is all part of the fun at the many local festivals.

Annunciation of the Virgin Mary – March 25.
Good Friday, Easter Sunday and Monday – moveable.
Labour Day – May 1.
White Monday – moveable.
Virgin Mary Dormit – August 15.
Thessaloniki only, local celebration – October 26.
National Celebration – October 28.
Christmas Day – December 25.
Virgin Mary – December 26.

What to bring back

All the resorts have souvenir and 'Greek art' shops, and most of what they stock is not particularly inspiring, unless your taste runs to imitations of classical pottery or miniature statues of Alexander the Great. On the other hand, determined bargain hunters can do well, and there's plenty of appealing local produce that's worth bringing back.

Clothes. Denim jeans, including Armani and Levis are often to be found in resort shops at lower prices than the UK. For good quality, fashionable clothes at reasonable prices, you have to go to Thessaloniki, and there, the choice is enormous.

Leather. You'll find belts and handbags everywhere more cheaply than at home, but if you want really top quality and design, you must expect to pay more.

Jewellery. Gold and silver is everywhere. The designs are sometimes a bit heavy and ornate, but there is some very nice stuff around too. Make sure you find out what carat you're buying as it may not always be marked.

Handicrafts. Hand-woven rugs are a good buy if you have the carrying capacity. You see small ones everywhere, but for the best choice, go to the mountain village of Arnea (see page 42). Table linen (especially lace and embroidered) is worth bringing back. Look for it in the markets in Thessaloniki and there are also some good shops in Ouranoupolis.

Food and drink. Dried herbs and spices from markets and supermarkets, honey, loukoumi (Greek delight), olive oil, nougat, salted almonds and pistachios, biscuits from a cake shop (zacharoplasteio) are all worth thinking about. Some people like to bring back bottles of ouzo or tsipouro, but personally I find that they tend to stay in the cupboard – somehow they don't taste the same back in cold, grey Britain. The same isn't true of the wine, though you'd do better to buy a couple of better quality bottles rather than several litres of plonk.

HALKIDIKI

A brief history *Prehistory and mythology.* There are two versions of the early history of Halkidiki – the mythological and the archaeological, and sometimes they actually overlap. The Ancients knew the region as Plegra – the Place of Fire – because it was believed to be the site of an epic battle between the Olympian gods, led by Zeus, and the Giants, the sons of Gea (Earth). A lot of rock-throwing went on. One of the giants was crushed by a boulder hurled at him by the gods, and was buried on Kassandra. Unfortunately, he wasn't dead at the time, and every so often he tries to struggle out from under the weight of rocks, causing earthquakes. The subsidence which affects the centre of the peninsula and the sulphur springs at Agia Paraskevi are present day signs of his continuing efforts!

The Athos peninsula was named after another of the giants, who threw a mountain at the gods, but missed his target, while Sithonia got its name from Sithon, son of the sea god Poseidon.

According to archaeologists, the Ancients were spot-on in their choice of name. Recent excavations at the Petralona Cave (see page 44) have shown traces of what is said to be the earliest known controlled fires, started by men around 700,000 years ago. The skull found in the cave is thought to belong to a person who lived there some 250,000 years ago, sharing the land with elephants and prehistoric animals now extinct.

Around 2000 BC, the many attractions of Halkidiki – fertile farming land, mineral deposits, ample forests and miles of coastlines – appealed as much to prehistoric man as they do to us today. There were settlements all round the coasts, as well as inland, and archaeologists have unearthed many artefacts from sites at Sani, Olynthos, Aphitos and Nikiti, to name but a few. The early inhabitants were probably from a variety of Hellenic tribes, lumped together by the Ancient Greeks as 'Thracians', because they thought they were people from Thrace in the far north.

The Persian War. It wasn't until around the eighth century BC that the population was expanded by the arrival of colonists from southern Greece – mainly from the city state of Halkis (the Halkideans – hence Halkidiki) and Eretria in Evvia. Other newcomers arrived from the island of Andros, Corinth and from Athens and began to build their cities. By the fifth century BC, the cities of Halkidiki got sucked into the ongoing struggle between the Persians and Athens and its allies, known as the Persian War. The historian Herodotus describes how the Persian fleet of 300 ships, led by the Emperor Darius' son Mardonius, came to a nasty end in a storm while trying to round the tip of the Athos peninsula. Some 30,000 men were lost, and it was this disaster which, in 480 BC, inspired Xerxes to cut a canal across the head of the peninsula at Nea Roda to prevent a recurrence of the tragedy. He went around forcing Halkideans to join his army and navy, supply him with ships and subsidise his military campaigns, so it's hardly surprising that when the Greeks defeated the Persians at the naval battle of Salamis, Halkidiki took the opportunity to rebel against the Persians. One of the results was a siege of the city of Olynthos, after which the Persians killed all the inhabitants.

Philip and Alexander. Peace didn't last long, however, and Halkidiki became involved in the Peloponnesian Wars between Athens and Sparta, and then in the ensuing power struggle with King Philip II of Macedonia (Philip of Macedon). Unfortunately for them they ended up on the losing side, and the cities of the Halkidean League were crushed by Philip's armies in 348 BC. The city of Olynthos was destroyed, and Halkidiki was incorporated into the Macedonian Empire. The Athenian orator Demosthenes made famous speeches to try and persuade the Athenians of the need to defend Olynthos, but by the time the citizens finally succumbed to his persuasion, it was already all over.

Halkidiki was then part of the great Macedonian Empire of Philip and his even more successful son Alexander the Great – whose glory is reflected in the exhibits in the Archaeological Museum of Thessaloniki (see page 48). In fact, Thessaloniki itself, established in 316 BC by the Macedonian King Kassander, was named after his wife Thessaloniki, sister of Alexander, while the king gave his own name to the peninsula we know as Kassandra.

The Romans. The next battles were with the Romans, and in 168 AD, the whole of Macedonia was conquered by them, and subsequently became part of the Byzantine Empire. This didn't mean the people benefited from the famous Roman Peace, however, as successive waves of barbarian tribes invaded the area and caused enormous devastation. Not only the Goths and the Huns, but later the Franks and the Catalans combined with pirates attacking by sea to contribute to the plunder and destruction.

The monks of Athos. During these years when attack from outside was so common, the influence of the monastic communities on Athos was spreading in the rest of Halkidiki. The Byzantine emperors made many grants of land to the monasteries, and between the ninth and fifteenth centuries, farming of cattle, grain and vines was developed under the protection of the 'metochia' – dependencies of the monasteries. It is from this time that the various towers scattered around Halkidiki date – you can see good examples in Nea Fokea, Ouranoupolis, Ierissos and Sani, for example. The inhabitants tended to congregate inland, away from the danger of pirates, and some of the older villages such as Parthenonas, Nikiti,

Monks are still living the traditional life in the many monasteries of Mount Athos.

Agios Nikolaos and Gomati, for example, can probably date their origins back to this period.

The Turks. Apart from relatively short periods in the thirteenth and fourteenth centuries when Halkidiki was ruled by the Serbian Kingdom and then the Venetians, the next real threat was from the Turks. After various skirmishes, the Turks completed their conquest of the whole of Macedonia in 1430, where they were to remain for many centuries.

While we can assume that the local people were none too happy about this, there is evidence that for much of this time, the prosperity of the area increased. The Turks reorganised the mines and created new settlements to exploit them while the southern population concentrated on agriculture, still under the auspices of the Athos 'metochia'. Pirate raiding continued, however, and some people believe that the local inhabitants were not above joining in from time to time.

Revolt and revolution. The first real threat to the Turkish rule, however, did not appear until 1821, when the Greek Revolution began. As far as Halkidiki was concerned, it started in Poligiros, under the leadership of Emmanuel Papas, who organised his troops from a base inside Athos. However, despite early successes, the poorly armed people were defeated by November 1821, and the expected retribution was indeed terrible. Poligiros, along with dozens of other villages and the metochia were burned, and the inhabitants tortured and killed. One estimate suggests that as many as 10,000 were put to death, while others were sold into slavery, although many women and children escaped by boat to the islands. There were two more unsuccessful attempts to get rid of the Turks, in 1854 and 1878, before success finally came in 1912. This union with the rest of Greece led to another dramatic change in the fortunes of Halkidiki. In 1921, there was an exchange of populations between it and the Asia Minor area of Turkey. The Turks who had remained after 1912 left, while the many Greek families who had been living in Asia Minor, as well as others from Bulgaria and Thrace came to settle in Halkidiki. It is this great population movement, involving many thousands of people, which greatly influenced aspects of present-day culture. The most immediately obvious is in place names: many incomers named their new villages after their old ones – Neos Marmaras is one example – and brought their customs and cooking with them.

In the mountains

Map B2   **POLIGIROS**

This inland town, 500 m above sea level, nestling at the base of Mount Holomon and some 69 km from Thessaloniki, is the capital of Halkidiki. You can get there by bus from all the resorts, and the journey takes you through some interesting villages and beautiful countryside as the road climbs up to the town. With a population of around 4,500, it is a busy but welcoming place, and, although it makes relatively few concessions to tourists, is interesting to visit to see what 'real' local life is like.

The buses stop in the 18 Octobriou Square, and there's usually room to park there or in the streets around the post office. At the baker in the main road near the square, you can choose from a mouthwatering range of cakes and pastries – the baklavas is light and flaky and literally dripping with honey. No one will mind if you take them to the little bar opposite, where you can order a drink, and sit at one of the tiny tables outside, perched up on the concrete platform leaking honey all over the place.

Suitably fortified, it's worth making your way up the hill past the post office and the building with the yellow OTE signs to find the new town museum, the **Poligiros Museum**, next to the school. It is quite small but modern and very well laid-out. The best-known exhibit is the 'kouros', a half-finished statue of a young man dating from the sixth century BC which was found in the sea near Stagira. More to my taste, however, were the exhibits relating to everyday life – tiny terracotta figures from the Andrian colony of Akanthos (on the site of present-day Ierissos at the top of the Athos peninsula). They're rolling dough, using a pestle and mortar and there's a little sailing boat too – all dating from the sixth century. I also liked the gold jewellery from the third and fourth century, and a big sarcophagus, again from the excavations at Akanthos, which is painted with panthers, a lion, a bull and a pattern of plants.

Open Monday to Saturday 9 a.m. to 3 p.m. entrance 400 drachmas.

The buildings in the upper part of the town are uninspiring to say the least, but in the older parts there are plenty of examples of traditional Macedonian architecture. In the old quarter, the upper storeys of the house overhang the lower, with attractive carved wooden gables. It's often either cloudy or very hazy up in the mountains, but if you chance to be there on a clear day, it's worth climbing the Profitis Elias hill to the north-east of the town to see the distant prongs of the three Halkidiki peninsulas in the sparkling sea far below. (See Walking, page 20).

Tiberius II
(R)S

Generally, pizza restaurants feature infrequently in this guide, but the one next door to the museum deserves a mention. For one thing, there aren't that many places to eat in Poligiros, and for another, the pizza I had here was home-made and utterly delicious. Served piping hot from the oven, it featured spicy sausage, bacon, mushrooms, green peppers, tomatoes and masses of bubbling cheese. This, plus a beer, was only 1,300 drachmas. The surroundings are modern and lacking in character, but the place is sparkling clean and the centre of many comings and goings which entertain you while you eat. When I was there, the rain was coming down in stair-rods, but on a better day, you can sit at one of the tables outside on a raised concrete platform looking down over the road and beyond to the hills. The staff don't have much English, but they and the other customers are friendly and anxious to be helpful, so communication is usually possible in the end.

Epicouros
(R)M

You'll find this restaurant in the central square, down the hill past the church and opposite the bank. You go down the steps to find the tables set out under the trees, away from the noise and bustle of the town. It's a very peaceful and welcoming place, and the menu lists the 'specials' in English. You'll get more of a choice if you're there in July or August – the majority of customers are Greeks and that's when they come. I was sorry that an interesting-sounding sausage casserole wasn't available, but there was still plenty to choose from: various pastas, chops and steaks, beef in red sauce and stuffed aubergines, to name but some. As most people will probably be in Poligiros in the daytime, this is a good opportunity to have moussaka, which is usually cooked fresh for lunchtime. It was made with both potatoes and aubergines, with a lovely light cheese sauce on top. The stuffed tomatoes and peppers were very good too – not overcooked and well flavoured with fresh herbs. The beetroot salad here was the best we found – prepared as it should be with the leaves included and served with skordalia – garlic sauce. It was also the cheapest meal we had, and not just because we only drank water – just 2,200 drachmas for two.

Map A3 **ARNEA**

Some 38 km along the lovely mountain road from Poligiros is the pretty town of Arnea, which is on the bus routes from all the peninsulas and from Thessaloniki. As you approach, you get fantastic views of the countryside, down over the plain spread out below you. There are vines and all kinds of crops in the fields, plus goats with tinkling bells, sheep and chickens wandering across the road and, here and there, people working in the fields. The buses all stop in the little main square – you can park there too – and outside one of the cafés is a board giving details of the bus timetables so you can plan your return journey.

There are several pavement cafés in the square, most of them the traditional 'kafeneio' kind where the old men of the village sit to chat to their friends, play chess and backgammon and watch the world go by. If they're fully occupied, or you don't feel comfortable invading their territory, the café in the bottom right-hand corner of the square (where the bus timetable is) would be a good choice. You can sit at one of the tables on the raised paved patio and soak up the atmosphere. From your vantage point, you have a good view of the narrow, hilly streets, paved with cobbles and lined with lovely old houses. Many have wooden shutters and balconies laden with bright flowers and some covered in vines and flowering creepers.

You'll also see bright woven rugs hanging over many of the balconies to air – they are hand-woven in the village as they have been for centuries in the traditional styles. Around the square are three or four little shops where the owners are only too willing to show you some of their huge selection of rugs and runners, explaining about the dyes and the way they are made. Reds, blues, black and white are the predominant colours and there's every shape and size under the sun. Although they are mostly traditional designs, I did see one with the ubiquitous slogan 'Macedonia is Greek for ever' woven into it in Greek! As well as rugs, the shops have a selection of hand-made ethnic-type sweaters which are likely to be hard-wearing although they aren't exactly the last word in fashion. There are several bakers and cake shops selling the usual selection of honey and nut-based pastries, as well as very good bread and cheese or spinach pies, but there isn't really anywhere to have a meal. Down the cobbled road from the square, there's a little shop selling many kinds of locally produced honey. It is said that the

The charming mountain village of Arnea.

tree honey has the best flavour, and it's certainly delicious, but I couldn't resist the jars of walnut honey which has actual walnut chunks set in it, and goes perfectly with Greek yoghurt. Young women are supposed to buy it to feed to their husbands

In the mountains

or boyfriends – but attempts to find out why were met with blushes and giggles, so you can draw your own conclusions.

Map B1   PETRALONA CAVE

Open 9 a.m.–5 p.m. daily; entrance 700 drachmas
This features in most of the excursion schedules run by both tour operators and local travel companies as one of the sights to see. It's in the foothills of Mount Katsika, some 20 km from Nea Moudania. To get there, you drive through some lovely countryside with patchwork fields and olive groves and crops and animals visible among the hills. I had the privilege of being shown round in solitary splendour, because I visited it in May when it was raining very heavily and no one else had been foolish enough to venture out. Certainly, in those conditions it was very atmospheric, and not too difficult to imagine the lives of the humans who lived there around 700,000 years ago. The caves themselves are impressive, with amazing formations of red rock shaped into stalactites and stalagmites, but for me the most interesting aspect was the traces and reconstructions of human occupation. Some years ago, a human skull was found inside, thought to be that of a woman aged around twenty-five who probably lived (and died) over 250,000 years ago. Interestingly, there are signs that she suffered from a complaint familiar to most of us – tooth decay. There is now a reconstruction of how the body would have been lying. Archaeologists have also created a small scene of three model humans, gathered round a fire chewing on animal bones which is a bit gruesome but horribly fascinating. On the way out, you pass rows of glass cases displaying various objects found in the caves – bones, teeth and stone tools, plus models of some of the animals such as wild bears which would have been around when the caves were occupied.

Outside, there is a café, but as it was still raining like Noah's flood, I didn't get the chance to try it. In better weather, it would be a very peaceful place to sit and survey the lovely countryside around, provided that you didn't go at a too busy time.

Map B2   ANCIENT OLINTHOS

Some 10 km off the main coast road east of Gerakini, you'll find the ruins of what was once a thriving city before it was effectively destroyed by Philip of Macedon in 348 BC (see page 37). Unfortunately from our point of view, he and his army did such a thorough job that you need quite a lot of imagination to visualise the lives of the 30,000 or so people who once lived there. Today, what you see is two huge, flat-topped mounds, with traces of where the streets once ran, and the odd mosaic here and there. The views round about, however, are magnificent, especially in spring and early summer when the wild flowers are a dazzling rainbow of colour as far as the eye can see. Down below, there are olive groves and on the hills, straight lines of vines, with the odd tractor moving slowly across the fields. In the distance, you can look across the sea to Turtle Island and the misty outlines of Sithonia peninsula. On the way back down to the road there are two buildings, apparently housing a tiny museum and a bar, but as neither were open in May when I was there and there was no one around, I can't report on them.

Thessaloniki

Greece's second city is quite different from Athens, but has its own very real attractions. In terms of history, its glories are of the Byzantine rather than the classical era, but it's also a sophisticated modern city of around a million inhabitants in a beautiful setting.

You won't pass through it if you travel to Halkidiki direct from the airport, which is on the eastern outskirts, but it's simple enough to get there by bus from any of the holiday resorts. The terminal is just off Egnatia Odos, one of Thessaloniki's main arteries, but it's a long (and none too scenic) walk to the centre. The best bet is to get a taxi which shouldn't cost much more than 1,000 drachmas. Ask to be taken either to the White Tower or to Aristotelous Square, which are both good starting points for exploration.

Driving in from Halkidiki means a rather boring trek through the eastern outskirts before you reach the centre, but it's a good wide road. As traffic tends to move rather slowly, you have plenty of time to look where you're going and watch out for signposts.

Theoretically, you can't park right in the centre of Thessaloniki, and although people do, it's not to be recommended. There are signs to show you on which streets parking is permitted, as well as parking meters on many streets – 100 drachmas per hour. There is a free car park behind the White Tower museum if you can't find a convenient roadside spot.

Depending on how much time you have and where your interests lie, you can plan to concentrate on history and culture, shopping or, of course, eating and drinking. With an

Yachts sail close to Thessoloniki's famous White Tower Museum.

early start and plenty of stamina, you could easily get a taste of all three elements.

The modern city is spread out around the coastline, and in general, the areas of most interest to visitors are concentrated between the port at one end and the White Tower museum at the other. Peaceful it isn't because of the constant throb and hooting of traffic, but many of the streets have arcades over the pavement where you can walk in the shade, window-shopping to your heart's content. There are also a number of squares dotted around which are surprisingly quiet, with outdoor cafés offering a pleasant oasis of calm amidst all the action. Aristotelous, coming off the seafront road towards the harbour end is the biggest and best known, and the Greek Tourist Board information office is there. Several cafés have tables under the trees in the centre of the square, and it's a good place to stop and catch your breath. Navarinou Square, behind the White Tower off Tsimiski is small and relatively undiscovered – by tourists at least – but in the evenings the tavernas and bars are crowded with local people, with only the odd car trying to squeeze through now and then. You can get drinks and ice creams from kiosks by the White Tower – where there's also a public loo – and from the cafés in the park behind the Tower in front of the Archaeological Museum.

Shopping Shopaholics can indulge themselves to the full – especially if clothes, shoes, handbags and jewellery are their particular weaknesses. You'll do best to concentrate on a relatively small section bounded roughly by the streets called Nikis (the seafront road), Venizelou, Ermou and Agia Sofias. Shoes are a very good bet. You can find bargains, but in general the quality and designs are good, and although not inexpensive, the prices are cheaper than at home for the equivalent items. It's the same story with clothes – fashionable, well-made styles that are a bit different but rarely at the lower end of the price range. In both cases, it will be a lot easier if you know your continental sizes. You probably won't bother to sample the wares at the branches of BhS and Marks and Spencers – the clothes are what you'd expect, but apparently Greek women in particular love the quality and especially the undies!

Many shops accept credit cards, and there is a big post office on Tsimiski near Aristolelous Square where you can change currency, travellers' cheques and Eurocheques. *It is open from 7.30 a.m. to 8 p.m. Monday to Friday; 7.30 a.m. to 2 p.m. Saturdays and 9 a.m. to 1.30 p.m. Sundays. Generally shops are open from 8.30 a.m. to 3 p.m. Monday, Wednesday and Saturday, 8.30 a.m. to 2 p.m. and 5 p.m. to 8.30 p.m. Tuesday, Thursday and Friday, closed all day Sundays.* This means you have a long gap in the middle for lunch and to fit in any other sightseeing.

Even if shopping isn't your idea of fun, you would probably still enjoy a visit to Thessaloniki's lively food markets. The smaller one has more variety in terms of food, while the other is more general, with clothes, fabric, linen and the like as well. The first one is just a short walk from Aristotelous Square. The stalls and open-fronted shops are collected in a few narrow streets in the area to the left of Aristotelous where it meets Egnatia. The displays vary from the colourful to the mildly gruesome – the butchers' wares look rather gory to anyone accustomed to the sanitised offerings of a British supermarket. At the other extreme, however, the displays of fruit and vegetables are dazzling in their colours and varieties, and you'll also find great slabs of freshly made white cheeses, fish in all shapes and sizes, and more kinds of olives than you ever imagined existed. The stalls selling herbs and spices can be located by the aromatic smells, and the tiny packs of all kinds of strange and wonderful things are a treasure trove for cooks.

Less practical buys for the airline passengers are the big woven baskets, but this is a good place to find loukoumi (Greek delight) and halvas, the sweet concoction which comes in many different flavours and is usually sold in tins. The noise is terrific, with stallholders shouting their wares, local shoppers arguing about price or quality and you'll almost certainly be offered unrepeatable bargains by hopeful vendors. It's all good fun and very entertaining, even if you don't buy anything.

The other, more general market is in the square and narrow streets behind the Rotonda, in the area where the streets called Ethnikis Aminis and Agiou Dimitriou meet. There are little junk stalls – almost like a car boot sale, 'ethnic style' jewellery sellers and loads of lovely table linen as well as fantastic displays of fruit and veg that look like still life compositions. There are some good herb and spice stalls as well: the stuff is in big containers and you buy it by the cupful, with the measuring cups ready in each. The stallholders and other customers fall over themselves to explain to you what they are and how good – and the smells make them irresistible. Take home a packet of rigani for instance and you'll be reminded of your holiday every time you open it. And when you've had enough, there is quite a nice place to have a coffee or a frappé (iced coffee) on your left as you come out of the market on to Agiou Dimitriou.

Sightseeing

Museums. You can see the main attractions in the course of a quite comfortable stroll. The two main museums – the Archaeological and the White Tower are within a few minutes' walk of each other right at the eastern end of the commercial district.

You can't miss **The White Tower** which is a useful landmark as well as being worth a visit on its own account. In a series of small rooms leading off a stone spiral staircase, there are icons and other artefacts from the Byzantine period between 300 and 1430 AD. Although the building itself dates from the sixteenth century, and was once part of the city's defences, it has been renovated and turned into a well laid-out museum with a tiny café and viewing area at the top.

Opening hours: Mon. 12.30 p.m.–7 p.m., Tues.–Fri. 8 a.m.–7 p.m., Sat. and Sun. 8.30 a.m.–3 p.m.; after October 15 Mon.

The statue of local hero Alexander The Great in Thessaloniki.

10.30 a.m.–5 p.m., Tues.–Fri. 8 a.m.–5 p.m., Sat. and Sun. 8.30 a.m.–3 p.m., entrance 500 drachmas.

The Archaeological Museum is a new building, almost hidden behind trees, in HANTH (or YMCA) Square, up the road called **Germanou** from the White Tower. Although there are finds from northern Greece dating from prehistoric to Roman times, most visitors come to see the exhibits from the royal tombs of Vergina dating from the fourth century BC. Excavated in 1977–8, the tombs are believed to have held the remains of Philip of Macedon. The treasures are now housed in a special wing of the museum, and are quite stunning. The finely decorated gold casket held bones believed to be those of Philip, and the star on the lid was the emblem of the kings of Macedonia. Nowadays, it's known in Greece as the star of Vergina and is an important national symbol. The two oak wreaths made of gold are fantastically intricate and delicate and you simply have to see them to appreciate how beautiful they are. Even if you're not remotely interested in history or archaeology, these and the other gold jewellery from the same period should not be missed. Rather more down-to-earth but equally fascinating are the iron helmet – complete with plume and earflaps – and the iron and gold cuirass, the Macedonian equivalent of a bullet-proof vest found with other armour in the Great Tomb of Vergina. Among the collection of miniature ivory heads are two which are thought to be those of Philip and Alexander himself.

If you want to, you can see the whole wing in an hour, and there's rather a nice café round the corner to refresh yourselves afterwards.

Opening hours: Mon. 11.30 a.m.–6 p.m., Tues.–Fri. 8 a.m.–6 p.m., Sat. 8.30 a.m.–3 p.m., Sun. 8.30 a.m.–6 p.m., after October 15 Mon. 10.30 a.m.–5 p.m., Tues.–Fri. 8 a.m.–5 p.m., Sat. 8.30 a.m.–3 p.m., Sun. 8 a.m.–5 p.m.; entrance 1,000 drachmas.

Incidentally, you only have to read the labels on the exhibits to realise that Philip and Alexander still have great political significance today. The whole tenor of the historical explanations is that the Macedonian kingdom was GREEK, and the point is to emphasise that this area and its people, not to mention the very name Macedonia, are and always have been part of Greece. The twelve-pointed Star of Vergina accompanies the slogan you see everywhere from the airport to the paper bags they put your postcards into in shops: Macedonia is Greek forever. This is all related to the long-standing political rivalries in the Balkans, and in particular today to the disagreements with the part of Yugoslavia which its inhabitants call Macedonia and which the Greeks call Skopje. Anyone interested in delving further into this perennial and deeply felt debate might like to visit the **Museum of the Macedonian Struggle** just along to the seafront from the White Tower towards the port.

The Byzantine Museum is new, and in early 1995 contained a small collection of icons dating from the fifteenth to the nineteenth centuries. Other exhibits are being planned. You'll find it on Leoforou Stratou behind the Archaeological Museum.

Opening hours: Mon.–Fri. 5–9 p.m., Sat. 10–2 p.m. and 5–9 p.m., Sun. 10–2 p.m., entrance free.

Churches. The basilica of **Agia (St) Sophia** (up the street of the same name behind the Macedonian Struggle museum), founded in the eighth century, is a smaller version of its namesake in Istanbul. Inside, you can see mosaics and wall paintings from the ninth and tenth centuries, including a fine mosaic of the Virgin behind the altar. From 1430 until 1912,

Subtly coloured mosaics are a feature of the many Byzantine churches.

during the Turkish occupation, it was used mostly as a mosque, but now it has returned to its original role as an important centre of Greek Orthodoxy.

Agios Dimitrios (on Agiou Dimitriou, up towards the old town) is named after the Roman officer who was martyred for his Christianity during the persecutions by the Emperor Diocletian in the fourth century. In the twelfth century, invading Normans from Sicily stole the saint's relics from the church and took them away to Italy. In 1978, they were returned from the Monastery of San Lorenzo near Rimini, and are now housed in a new reliquary. During World War I, there was a serious fire in the district which raged for three days and destroyed the upper part of the church, as well as 70,000 homes. The top of the church was rebuilt, but you can still see many of the early mosaics and frescoes inside, and the remains of the Roman baths where Dimitrios was martyred, outside.

Other sites. As you walk around the city, you'll come across several ruins from the Roman era although there's nothing of any great significance. The Galerian Arch – or rather, the remains of it – has carved on it scenes from the Roman emperor's wars against the Persians, while the site of his palace is below in Navarinou Square. The nearby Rotonda, with its early mosaics and sculptures was intended as Galerius' final resting place. Near the upper end of Aristotelous Square are the remains of the old Roman agora (a meeting and market place), where you still find stalls selling bits and pieces, cheap jewellery and other knick-knacks, and local teenagers gathering in groups to meet their friends and chat.

The old town. Often known as the **Ano Poli** (or Upper City), the old town lives up to both its names. You can walk up to it from the lower city, but I wouldn't recommend it unless you're seriously energetic, and even then not if the weather is at all hot. The narrow streets leading up to it are phenomenally steep, and there are several series of stone steps to negotiate too. Unless you are particularly keen to see the old churches of Profitis Ilias and Ossios David on the way up, it's much better to take a taxi which will only cost around 500 drachmas.

The contrast strikes you forcefully coming up from the humming city below. Up here, it's all narrow streets with old houses, their flower-laden balconies almost touching. There's washing hung out in gardens, and people going about their everyday business unconscious of the appeal their area has for visitors. There are a couple of cafés where you can get a drink, and in the little square on your right just inside the main gate, there's a nice taverna for lunch. It's not an enormous menu, but the fried mussels were fresh, very hot and delicious, while the mixed fish dish was tasty and good value. Two main dishes like this, plus a couple of salads and beers or soft drinks come to around 3,000 drachmas.

For most people, the highlight of a visit to the old town is to see the old fourth century walls which were built to enclose and protect it, and to look out over them at the great city spread out below. At last you get a real idea of its size, and you can see tiny ships right out at sea – it's a spectacular view and well worth seeing. The best spot is a specially built viewing platform on the road above the upper town. You follow the signs to the Hotel Phillipeion, and when you can see it above you to the right, there's a little track off to the left which takes you into the parking area. Ahead of you, up the stone steps, there are wooden shelters with seats in front of the walls where you can sit and look down on the city spread out before you.

Thessaloniki

Eating and drinking. In the lower town, you have a good choice of cafés where you can go for hot or cold drinks, ice cream and sometimes pastries, and some also offer light meals and snacks. Along Nikis, the seafront street, you have the advantage of a lovely view, but the noise and fumes of the constant stream of traffic dilute the charm somewhat. Nevertheless, they are popular with local people, and it can be fun to watch the comings and goings as new arrivals greet their friends, and chairs and tables are reorganised to accommodate them. Those favoured by the student types just along from the Harley Davidson dealer are particularly chaotic and quite good fun.

ark cafés

Between the Archaeological Museum and the White Tower is a huge park, the centre of which is a succession of open air cafés, running into one another with tables and chairs crowded alongside the path and under the trees. Prices for drinks and snacks are lower here, and it's a peaceful place to sit away from the worst of the bustle and traffic noise. Mostly used by Greek customers, they do however have menus in English which can provide a certain amount of amusement in themselves. 'Ration', for instance, is defined as 'sausage boiled' or 'sausage roasted', 700 drachmas, while 'fish toe salad' is a mere 400. Several places offer a glass of ouzo plus titbits (sometimes called 'pikilia ouzo') for around 450 to 600 drachmas. There's a good selection of ice creams available too, plain and specialities, including kadaifi for 600 drachmas, as well as pastries. Kadaifi is a nut-filled pastry made with thin strands like vermicelli and soaked in honey, which is often served with ice cream. Prices are much of a muchness, as are the menus, so you may as well just pick the one you like the look of and you won't go far wrong. At the end nearest the White Tower there's a pretty fountain, overlooked by the last of the cafés on either side.

If you find yourself at the other end of town and in need of a drink, there are several very attractive cafés on the right-hand side of Aristotelous Square as you turn in from the sea, close to the Tourist Information Office. They're less noisy and crowded than the ones on the seafront itself, with comfortable seats away from the traffic. Prices are higher than in the park, however, as they tend to cater mostly for tourists.

At the top right-hand corner of the square, just past the Tourist Office, there's a brilliant patisserie which gives off the most tempting baking smells. It's a good source of unusual gifts for sweet-toothed friends – the marzipan fruits are a work of art. You can choose your own selection, or buy them in pre-packed clear boxes from 1,600 drachmas.

If you're visiting Agia Sophia or shopping in Tsimiski, there is a lovely little pedestrianised street running from Tsimiski up to the church where you can stop for coffee or a snack. Called Iktinou, it's quiet and shady, overhung with trees and full of flowering shrubs.

The Café do Brasil
(R)M

The Café do Brasil has plain white canvas umbrellas, and serves a good variety of ice creams, although it's not particularly cheap. A frappé (iced coffee) and chocolate ice cream, for example, cost 1,800 drachmas, but they're lovely.

Tiffany's
(R)S

Tiffany's is a steak and chips place with fast service, reasonable prices, and a favourite haunt of young Thessalonikians in the evenings.

Restaurant Tottis
(R)S

At the bottom left-hand corner of Anstotelous square, where it meets Nikis, this restaurant has tables on the pavement plus masses of room inside and a bustling atmosphere quite distinct from the slower-paced village tavernas. It's a good choice for snack meals, with ample Greek salads, toasted pitta bread sandwiches (served with crisps) at very reasonable prices. There's a selection of pastas for around 1,000 drachmas, plus soups and starters at about 600. Inside on a busy lunchtime, it felt more like being in a pub than a restaurant – except that you don't have to queue at the bar!

Ouzeri Tottis
(R)S

Next door, as you go into the square proper, the Ouzeri Tottis has an interesting selection of mainly seafood dishes, such as anchovies with rigani, boiled mussels, stuffed squid and swordfish. It's an attractive location, but as a result prices aren't cheap – you could easily spend 6,000 on lunch for two.

Aristotelous Ouzeri
(R)L *8, Aristotelous St*

It's a bit hard to spot as there's no sign on the outside, but you'll find it opposite the building with the big neon Microsoft sign, or you can simply ask a taxi to take you there as it's very famous. You go through an archway with brass plaques saying the German school is inside, but don't be put off by this. Straight ahead, there's a little courtyard with tables crammed into every available space outside and in, and crowded with local people and waiters rushing round with loaded trays. You may have to wait for a table at busy times – and lunch extends well into the afternoon – but it's worth it in the end. There is an English menu, but some of the waiters speak English too and are happy to advise or recommend specialities if you ask. That was how I came to try galeos saganaki – small pieces of white fish in a mild mustard sauce – and stuffed soupia (or cuttlefish), filled with feta, tomato and green peppercorns – both utterly mouthwatering. Halves of baked potato topped with cheese, white beans baked in the oven with tomatoes and herbs, tzatziki and fried red peppers completed a gluttonous lunch for two, which, with a half bottle of good white wine, came to 6,850 drachmas. Ouzo and tsipouro are good here too, and those with a sweet tooth might like to try baked halva served with lemon which is reckoned to be excellent. A taste of the real Greece, and well worth seeking out.

Zappeo
(R)S

Just off Ethnikis Aminis in a little street called Alex Svolou on the right going uphill, is a good choice for a quick and reasonably priced lunch. It's near the university and popular with students but closed in the evenings. There are about ten tables on the pavement outside, where you can sit and watch the world go by. A good selection of Greek cooking – papoutsaki consisted of courgettes (not aubergines as advertised on the menu) stuffed with mince and tomato sauce and topped with a cheese sauce (700 drachmas); other options included baked fish with onions and garlic (750), meatballs from the oven (700) and a casserole of country sausages with sweet green peppers (700).

Ta Nisia (The Islands)
(R)L *13, Proxenou Koromilia St   031-285 995*

Proxenou Koromilia runs immediately behind and parallel to Leoforos Nikis.

The blue and white decor of this charming two-storey taverna makes it feel like you actually are in one of the Cyclades Islands, and it can get very crowded later in the evening when the local people come out to eat. It's one of the few places where you would be wise to book, although it isn't essential. The menu is absolutely vast, with a particularly good choice of seafood – shrimps for example are served in four ways: with bacon, in sauce, with cream and shrimp cocktail. You can also get game (classified as 'shoots') in season – hare with onions or wild pork, plus a big variety of steaks, chops and grilled or roast meat. The choice of starters and salads is almost overwhelming, and staples like melitzanosalata (aubergine dip) and taramosalata are very well made. There are some unusual desserts too – including roast quince and walnut pie – but you must have iron self-control or a huge appetite if you have room for anything more than fresh fruit. With a bottle of wine, expect to pay around 8,000 drachmas for two, depending on your choice of food.

Olymbos
(R)S

An unusual restaurant along by the harbour on Nikis that's particularly popular with lunching Greek businessmen. Inside, it's a vast cavern of a room which looks as though it has been more or less untouched since some time in the 1930s. Wooden panelling on the walls covers a gallery which is no longer used, and there are faded pictures of Thessaloniki which have obviously been there for years. The menu is Greek, and while the staff give the impression that they don't see a lot of tourist customers, they are helpful and can manage enough English to get by. There's a good selection of the usual starters, and 'pilafi' – rice with mussels – is something of a speciality. Chicken with roast potatoes seemed popular with the businessmen and proved to be very good. In fact, the 'dish of the day' changes and is likely to be worth ordering if it happens to be something you like. A two-course lunch with beer should cost around 2,000 drachmas.

Ta Adelphia (The Brothers)
(R)M

This is one of a host of tavernas and bars overflowing on to the pavements around the edge of Navarinou Square. Like most of the others, it's only open in the evening, and although it's crowded, you shouldn't have any trouble getting a table. The atmosphere is busy and lively – one evening when I was there, a group of young Greeks obviously out celebrating burst into spontaneous singing and dancing, cheered on by the rest of the customers. Although not fancy, the food is good and quite reasonably priced, and the service is friendly. As well as the usual salads and starters, there were a few more unusual ones, such as spicy cabbage and the beetroot salad was very good. The lamb with oregano had a lovely aroma, and tasted good too, while the village sausages were full of garlic and spice and came with fresh golden chips. With retsina from the barrel which was actually quite drinkable at 600 drachmas for a half-litre jug, this was a pretty good dinner for two at 4,000 drachmas.

Taverna To Mouragio (The Haven)
(R)L   *Katouni 11–13*

This is one of several attractive tavernas in the Ladadika district at the western end of Tsimiski, just behind the harbour. This used to be the old olive market, and the once derelict shops and warehouses have now been converted into bars and tavernas lit by pretty lamps in a couple of narrow streets. With an unusual and interesting choice of salads and starters, it's an ideal place to go for a mezedes-style meal. Among my favourites are feta saganaki (cheese baked in foil with tomatoes and rigani), mussels saganaki (mussels in a peppery, creamy sauce), prawns saganaki (prawns with melted cheese and a hot seafood sauce) and courgette fritters. A selection like this, accompanied by a few salads such as aubergine, tzatziki and tomato and cucumber, make a delicious and surprisingly filling meal. If you still have room, the Turkish crème caramel slips down easily, or there's fresh fruit and pastries. With a bottle of retsina, the average price for two would be around 7–8,000 drachmas.

Mylos
(R)L   *Georgiou Andreou, off 26 Octobriou*

A whole complex offering just about everything in the way of entertainment, Mylos is behind the docks at the eastern end of town. All taxi drivers know it, and there are plenty waiting around to pick up departing customers. There's a kind of ticket office (tameio) at the entrance, where you pay 1,000 drachmas a head entry, which will be deducted from your final bill. Inside, it's all cobbles and red bricks converted from a derelict flour mill with tavernas, bars, exhibitions and live music all on offer in different areas of the complex. While it's rather trendy and very popular with younger Greeks, there's something for everyone and it's open during the day as well as in the evenings.

Kassandra peninsula

Map C2 **NEA POTIDEA**

This is the village which you can see on either side below the main road as it crosses the canal at the top of the Kassandra peninsula. To your left is a small marina with fishing and pleasure boats, and a very nice sandy beach with cool clear water. Along the new pedestrianised paved promenade behind the beach, there are a few bars and a cake and coffee place, but they start closing up after the Greek tourists have departed at the end of August. To your right, under the bridge which carries the main road, you walk up a minor road to the village proper, which is charming. In the centre is a pretty square with flowering trees and a lovely fountain, with shops and a couple of tavernas around the edge.

Taverna Phillipos
(R)M

Overlooking the square, Taverna Phillipos has a cane roof over a paved patio, where you sit at outdoor table surrounded by flowering plants in tubs and troughs. You can stop just for a coffee or a drink, but if you want to eat, the menu offers fresh fish, octopus at 900 drachmas, shrimp salad for 1,000, fried pumpkin at 400 plus all the usual starters and main courses. The service is friendly and reasonably fast, and the Greek music not too loud. The village is very clean and neat and particularly well-kept – a lovely quiet spot to pause for an hour or two.

Artos café
(R)S

As you come back up on to the main road from the village side there's a very nice coffee and cake place on the corner – look for the Artos sign. Although there's a certain amount of traffic noise as it's on the main road, it also seems to be a general meeting place for the villagers as they pass by on their way home, to the shops or the bus stop opposite, which makes it a good spot for people-watching. The decor is very attractive, with green-painted wooden tables, white canvas directors' chairs under matching umbrellas on a little platform outside. Inside is a paradise for cake and pastry lovers, with a long sparkling clean glass cabinet full of a mouth-watering array of delicious concoctions. There are gâteaux, cream and chocolate cakes, a dozen kinds of biscuits plus a big selection of the honey and nut pastries to dither over. The charming young woman behind the counter was happy to explain what each one was made of, and you can eat there or take your purchases away – or, as we did, both.

Map C2 NEA FOKEA

A small and very attractive fishing village with a life of its own, Nea Fokea offers holidaymakers a real welcome without being too touristy. The local mayor Theologos is known locally as 'the flower man' because he shows his care for the natural environment in a very practical way by planting flowers and trees all round the village, and exhorting and cajoling his neighbours to do the same. You'll often see him around, checking on the state of his charges, and reminding villagers that their flower pots need watering. On a grassy hill above the beach, Nea Fokea has one of the area's remaining Byzantine towers, and from the nearby benches you can get a wonderful view of the misty hills of Sithonia and along the Kassandra coast. In the summer, there are occasional performances by visiting theatre groups in the small open-air theatre behind the tower – including Shakespeare plays in Greek! Look for posters around the village if you'd like to sample the experience. On the corner by the village traffic lights, you can see the miniature underground church of Agios Pavlos – St Paul – below the tiny blue and white building in a small courtyard opposite the beach tavernas. You have to bend low to get through the door into the entrance room, and from there a narrow tunnel leads into a big chamber where Holy Water is collected in a basin. The story is that St Paul was attacked while teaching in Ierissos, and made his escape underground, arriving by means of tunnels in Nea Fokea. The Holy Water appears at the spot where he emerged.

Across the road, you'll see a row of tavernas overlooking the beach where you can sit and watch the brightly coloured fishing boats coming and going.

Restaurant Kostis
(R)L

Definitely a cut above your average psarotaverna. On the road side, there are large traditional amphoras planted with flowers, and a few tables where local people gather to drink coffee and

Restaurant Kostis in Nea Fokea where the food is a real treat.

talk. The arched room of the main restaurant is attractively decorated in blue and white, and there are tables on a balcony outside looking out on to the tower and the sea. The chef takes great care with the starters and side dishes – which are delicious and attractively presented. Look for feta with red peppers and onions, grilled octopus, courgettes fried in thin golden slices and served with skordalia – the garlicky bread sauce which is seriously antisocial – and red peppers skinned and grilled on charcoal. Even everyday dishes like taramosolata and melitzanosalata are something special here. The former looks – and tastes – as though it's made from simple, natural ingredients, without that vivid orangey appearance suggestive of strange colourings and additives. The Greeks usually translate melitzanosalata as aubergine (or eggplant) salad, but we would probably call it a dip. It can be a bit slimy and tasteless in some places, but here it is made properly, with a rough texture and smokey taste that comes from the aubergines being grilled over charcoal first. If you can resist stuffing yourself to bursting at this stage, this is one of the places to splash out on fresh fish. The chef will explain what he has to offer on any particular day, and if you choose one of the large fish, it will be brought for you to see and approve before it is prepared and cooked. Alternatively, if you can't imagine what, say, beatle fish actually are, you'll be taken into the kitchen to see the day's offerings and choose for yourself. The cod fried in fine batter (vakalaos) and served with skordalia is especially good, and popular with the Greeks who flock there at lunchtimes. They will often have it with tsipouro – a clear spirit similar to the Cretan raki but with more a throat-friendly flavour which can delude you into thinking it's relatively innocuous. It is a local speciality, and brought to the table in a small glass jug, but remember to take plenty of water at the same time if you plan to walk out of the restaurant afterwards. The service is friendly but very professional and efficient, and the chitchat among friends and neighbours at the tables helps to create a very relaxing atmosphere. Kostis is more expensive than most tavernas – say 9,000 drachmas for two with a good bottle of wine – but if I were only going to have one meal out of my hotel in Kassandra, this is the place I'd choose.

There are two other tavernas in the same little block which share the same lovely views and are perfectly OK, if more ordinary. You can have the usual selection of salads, fish and main dishes such as souvlaki and freshly cooked golden chips plus beer or a soft drink for around 2–2,500 a head.

Map C2   SANI BEACH HOLIDAY RESORT

Ten kilometres off the main road at Nea Fokea, you come to Sani – a beautiful pine-covered cape with lovely beaches and stunning views. Described by its owners as 'a contemporary ecological holidays reserve', the complex is located in one of the last virgin areas of the Mediterranean, on the Emerald Peninsula.

The resort's facilities include the four-star Sani Beach Hotel, the Sani Beach Club (four-star), Sani Camping with space for 1200 guests and Porto Sani, which has an adjacent shopping centre and its own marina providing private moorings for crafts of all sizes. In addition, on the wooded hills above the sea, you'll see the Sani Villas, attractive and luxurious country houses built in a variety of architectural styles, blending the traditional with the contemporary.

Restaurants overlooking the sea are one of the delights of Halkidiki.

The hotel beaches have all the watersports facilities you could want for hire, the sand is clean and the water crystal clear. They are a bit off the beaten track, however, and you probably need transport or at least to hire a bike if you want to see any more of the area. The Sani Beach Hotel has a courtesy bus which will take you to Nea Fokea for a few hundred drachmas, where you can pick up the ordinary KTEL buses on the main road. Walking through the pine-scented countryside is a delight if it's not too hot, and one of the Hotel Association's marked walks (see pages 20–26) begins just behind the Sani Beach Hotel.

Sani Beach Hotel
(H)L

A large resort complex with 932 beds, the four-star hotel is one of the most sophisticated in Kassandra. I suspect many holidaymakers never venture very far from the complex, which

One of the attractive chalets in the Sani Beach Resort.

really is like a resort in miniature, with water sports, including a sailing and windsurfing centre, tennis courts, its own mini-shopping arcade, hairdresser and facilities for many other activities including archery, darts, aerobics and waterpolo. The hotel's 'animation team' put on regular shows in the theatre, and there's a nightclub/disco, regular live music in one of the bars, plus an à la carte taverna offering Greek cuisine. Within easy reach you'll find a 'pub' bar, where the drinks prices are lower than in the hotel. The menu in the main restaurant includes interesting Greek as well as international-style dishes, although I couldn't resist the huge variety of hot and cold buffet-style starters and so could rarely manage the main course. Although all the staff are friendly and helpful, the size of the place can't help but make it feel a little impersonal, but for those who like everything on hand, it's an excellent choice.

everything on hand, it's an excellent choice. And if you do want
to explore a bit further, there are bikes and mopeds for rent,
and an Atlas car hire desk in the reception area.

Sani Beach Phocea Club
(H)L

Just a 10-minute stroll from the Sani Beach Hotel and under
the same ownership, this is a four-star bungalow complex with
436 beds and beautifully landscaped gardens. Facilities include
an open-air theatre, brasserie and beach bar, disco and piano
bar, and a rather nice ouzeri. There's also the option of using
any of the facilities of the Sani Beach – there's a regular shuttle
bus between the two.

Paradise Simantro Beach
(H)L

This is primarily for sports enthusiasts and is used by the UK
operator Mark Warner as one of their holiday clubs. The low
buildings with their red-tiled roofs are laid out on three sides of
a courtyard around the pool, with the fourth side open to the
sea. The design is inspired by the architecture of the Athos
monasteries, and many of the buildings feature brightly
painted panels on stone or wooden walls. Inside the same
theme is picked up, with wooden furniture and locally made
rugs in the bedrooms and public rooms. There are facilities for
most sports, including six synthetic grass tennis courts, a small
shopping centre and a lovely beach overlooked by the hotel's
taverna. The surrounding pine woods make this a beautiful
location, but it is a bit cut off. Those who want to venture
further afield will either have to walk to the main road – around
12 km – or hire a mountain bike or a car, both of which can be
done from the hotel.

Map C2 **AFITOS**

One of the older villages in Kassandra which existed before the
influx of people from Asia Minor, Afitos (or Athitos as the
newer version has it) has expanded into quite a busy tourist
resort in recent years. You can get an impression of how life
used to be from the tiny **village museum** on the left of the main
street as you walk down towards the sea. Founded in 1975, it's
just the front room of a house, with a rather eccentric collection
of exhibits crammed into it. Most are agricultural implements

The traditional village of Afitos has many shops and tavernas.

of one kind or another, although since the labelling is somewhat erratic and mostly in Greek, you will have to work out for yourself what some of them were actually used for. On the table inside is a printed list of numbered exhibits in English to help you work out what you're looking at, although it still leaves a certain amount to the imagination. You can see a spinning wheel, and wooden reapers, together with a large impressive press and implements for separating stones from the wheat. On the walls are some fascinating old photos of people working in the fields, and even the relatively recent ones look as though they come from another, quite different world. All the exhibits were given by local families, and though it's a bit like the Old Curiosity Shop, the museum has real charm and does manage to convey something of village and agricultural life as it was. *Entry is free and completely unsupervised, but there's a collection box and a visitors' book by the door if you want to make a donation to the upkeep.*

The original village buildings were large and imposing, built of stone with thick walls and small windows. Some are now being restored, and there's a particularly fine example which has been turned by its young owner into a bar. You get to it by going up the narrow hill path at the bottom of the main street next to the Greek art shop. When I visited, it had no name, but you'll see it on your left just before the cliff. Inside it's shady with dark wood furniture, and there are a few tables outside where you can sit and enjoy the view. The friendly owner will be happy to tell you how he restored the 250-year-old house, and has turned it into a bar just to cover his costs, with no aim of making his fortune. It's not very big, so he probably won't, but it's well worth a visit.

Gastronomically, Afitos is something of a mixed bag, with the better tavernas up the minor road, parallel to the main street leading down from the coast road. With a supermarket and a tempting baker-cum-cake shop, it's a good place to pick up a picnic, and the tavernas all have a very friendly atmosphere, even those where the cooking is nothing out of the ordinary.

Café ouzeri
(R)S

No English sign but you'll find it off to the left of the main road near the square, opposite the car hire/tourist office place near the black and white EOT sign. Small and friendly and not too noisy, it offers the usual selection of souvlaki, grilled chicken, kalamaria, tzatziki and salads, but there's also good fried pale green peppers – hot and oily. Fairly inexpensive at around 2–3,000 drachmas for a main dish, a couple of starters and a salad and beer or local wine.

Bloody Marvellous taverna
(R)S

Bloody Marvellous taverna – as it's universally known from the banner stretched across the wall – is on the right-hand side of the main street near the baker. This is allegedly the general opinion among the (mostly British) clientele, and proudly displayed like the critics' notices you see stuck up outside theatres at home. The taverna decor is cheerful, with blue painted pillars under a wooden roof, tubs of plants and flowers on the tables, although the machine producing the rather cracked Greek music seemed to be in dire need of repair when

I was there. The food is freshly cooked and hot, if nothing very special. The stuffed tomatoes were pleasantly laced with fresh mint, but the meat in the veal and potatoes casserole wasn't particularly appetising, although the potatoes were. The chickens roasting on a spit looked and smelled good, but much of the taverna's undoubted popularity is probably down to the efficient and entertaining service. The waiters are prone to do an impromptu dance or burst into song as they serve your meal, and the place has a friendly and welcoming atmosphere. Prices are reasonable too – around 2,000 drachmas for a main course, salad and beer.

Taverna To Perasma (The Passage)
(R)M

This restaurant is on the minor road mentioned above and is a very good place to go if you want to try mezedes – the famous Greek equivalent of hors d'oeuvres which can be a wonderful meal in themselves. The sign outside invites you to explore the possibilities – and if you're unsure what or how much to order, the friendly Australian Greek staff will be only too happy to help you. Just give the waiter an idea of how much you want to spend, plus any particular likes or dislikes if you have them, and he will bring you a specially chosen selection of hot and cold mezedes. A typical spread might be sweet red pepper salad, soused anchovies in oil, hot white beans with herbs and tomatoes baked in the oven, tzatziki, fried kephalotiri cheese and aubergine imam – stuffed with spicy tomatoes and onion. This lot – enough for two – plus a bottle of retsina and Greek coffees would cost around 4,500 drachmas. They also offer main dishes if you prefer – lamb chops, souvlaki, chicken, various pastas and omelettes – plus, unusually, desserts including apple pie, ice cream and fruit salad.

Gastronomia
(R)M

Gastronomia is a smart-looking taverna just across the road and was certainly not short of customers. A sign outside announces that they specialise in 'Graeco-Italian cuisine' and it's a good option if you fancy something a little different from the usual taverna fare. Pasta is served very widely in Halkidiki – especially what's variously described as 'macarones' or spaghetti 'bolonez', but the types of pasta here were described as Greek specialities – two kinds of lasagne! Whether or not it's truly Greek, it certainly looked and tasted good and the service was fast and pleasant.

Taverna Vrachos (The Rock)
(R)M

The Taverna Vrachos is perched high up on a cliff overlooking the beach. You get to it by turning left along the side street from the main square. It's a quiet and peaceful spot with a stunning view and a good selection of fish on the menu. Fresh locally caught red mullet (barbounia) sounded expensive at 6,000 drachmas a kilo, but for one person, three reasonably sized fish, simply grilled with lemon, came to 1,500. One large and one small grilled fillet of sole were 1,200 – and delicious too. At around 3 p.m. on a Sunday, the place was popular with Greeks enjoying a family lunch – striped bass (lavraki) and what the menu called 'flatfish' (at 7,000 drachmas per kilo) looked inviting, but the huge platter of crayfish with lemons and herbs plus courgette fritters served to a neighbouring table was a work of art!

The beautiful old church of Afitos.

Beach café/bar
(R)S

On the beach itself is a tiny, charmingly scruffy and chaotic bar-cum-café. It looked as though it had been there for years, with few concessions to the advent of foreign holidaymakers. Rough wooden tables with blue painted wooden and rush chairs were scattered around, and there were old fishing nets weighted with conch shells hung from the trees. After sitting patiently for a while waiting for service that didn't materialise, we realised that more seasoned habitués were simply helping themselves to soft drinks or beer from the two large cold cabinets, then paying when someone noticed. A man looking like an ageing Greek hippy was cooking fish on a smokey barbecue, but it turned out to be his own lunch! The performance was then repeated by another local, with the same result, and as far as tourists were concerned, the dishes on offer seemed to be confined to Greek salad and chips – both of which looked very nice. It's a beautiful spot, and the comings and goings hugely entertaining, but the enticing smell of the apparently unobtainable fish finally drove us elsewhere in search of a more manageable system.

Hotel Aphytys
(H)M

In a lovely situation right on the beach and surrounded by gardens just 300 m from the village. There are 74 rooms, all with a balcony in an attractive low rise building. Facilities include a pool right by the beach, plus tennis, table tennis and water sports. You'll also find a restaurant and a bar/café and there is a lovely view out to sea.

Hotel Aristoteles Beach
(H)L

Just before you get to Afitos, about 2 km from Nea Fokea, you see an enormous sign suspended from a footbridge over the main road proclaiming the Hotel Aristoteles Beach. Look above and to the right, and there is the cluster of white, red-roofed buildings of the hotel, perched above the road and with spectacular views over the sea and the coastline. You reach the beach some 40 m below along the walkway and down steps, and there you'll find watersports facilities and a beach bar. As well as a mini-market, the hotel has an à la carte taverna where you can have lunch, tennis court and evening entertainments as well as a large, pretty garden area, so you need never venture further if you're content with what's on offer. However, you can get the bus on the main road, or the hotel runs its own courtesy bus service for a moderate charge into the village of Afitos some 2 km away.

Map C2 KALLITHEA

This is the largest and most commercialised resort in Kassandra and doesn't really have the feel of a genuine Greek village. Nevertheless, the local people are friendly and welcoming, and there's a good selection of shops and bars and several tavernas and cafés. There's also a 24-hour money change machine as well as a branch of the Ionian Bank where you can change travellers' and Eurocheques. Supermarkets, souvenir shops which sell British newspapers and books and several cafés and more-or-less fast food places are strung out along the main road, and you'll find more in the pedestrianised area just behind. There are several shops selling reasonably priced holiday-style clothes, Levi jeans at bargain prices, belts and the like and a couple of jewellers. On the opposite side of the road from the shopping area, there's a very pretty square, with palm trees, flowers and a fountain where you can sit on wooden benches and look out to sea or just watch the world go by for nothing. Kallithea gets very busy in high season, and the crossroads turns into a noisy mass of cars hooting, trying to park or simply get through the mêlée, but at other times it's less frantic.

The fine shingle beach is long but not very wide, and there are public showers by the tavernas. If you're longing for a good, old-fashioned British breakfast or even a pizza, you'll be spoilt for choice, but anyone wanting a taste of the real Greece will have more of a problem.

Café Louna
(R)S

Down a few steps from the left-hand corner of the square, perched on the edge of the cliff, this pretty café has a lovely view down the coastline. During the day, you can have coffee, drinks, rather good milkshakes, ice-cream, pastries plus sandwiches and 'tost' – a toasted sandwich with ham and cheese, rather like the French croque-monsieur. In the evening it's more of a bar serving a selection of exotically-named cocktails. There's always music in the background, but it's not deafening and it's a pleasant spot to while away the odd hour or two.

O Kostas
(R)S

Inside the pedestrian precinct, there's an excellent zacharoplasteio, a coffee and cake place with its sign in Greek only. To find it, walk up the road through the centre of the precinct, with Haris Taverna on your right, and you'll see it on your right next door to the shop called Chic fashion. There are several tables outside, with Greek customers usually in the majority, and the cakes are really lovely. Here you can get both bugatsa – the Halkidiki speciality (see page 28) – and loukoumades, the tiny honey-soaked doughnut-type mouthfuls which are utterly addictive. They also have baklavas and kadaifi – the shredded wheat one – plus revani, a cake made with semolina. It's another good place for people-watching – I sat there for ages, as the staff in the fast-food café opposite kept appearing with cages of birds and clambering around to hang them up on their appointed hooks under the awning, which seemed to require a great deal of loud debate, even though it's presumably a daily occurrence.

If you want to find a taverna with reasonable food and a bit of Greek atmosphere, there are a few worth trying.

Taverna Elena
(R)S

At the far end of the street with Artos bakery on the corner, through the centre of the precinct – is quiet and simple, and away from the main buzz. As well as the standard fare, it offers swordfish, moussaka and a good selection of salads and is not too expensive.

Ouzeri Paramithi
(R)S

Ouzeri Paramithi is on the main road, the first taverna you come to on the right-hand side as you come into Kallithea from the north, opposite the Atlas car hire office. It has more of a Greek feel than most of the other places in the resort, and the souvlaki is tasty and relatively inexpensive at 1,300 drachmas. If you're longing for something to get your teeth into, you might try the steak with garlic butter, 1,900, and the swordfish is good too.

Kassandra peninsula

Aethrion taverna
(R)S

> Next door to the Ouzeri Paramithi, this restaurant is rather pretty, with lots of trees and flowering plants to screen the tables from the passing traffic. Here you can sample the fried mussels which are a speciality of Halkidiki for 550 drachmas, or mussels in sauce for 950. Stuffed squid is good too, or for something a bit different, there's chicken croquettes at 700 drachmas.

Face taverna
(R)S

> This is in the precinct just behind Chris motor bike hire and offers a couple of set meals which give you the chance to try a number of different Greek dishes at a reasonable price. The 'fish plate Afroditi' consists of shrimp, squid, fish fillet, chips, vegetables, green salad and rice plus a Greek brandy or ouzo for 3,000 drachmas; the 'village plate Olympos' offers doner and shish kebabs, rice, vegetables, Greek salad, garlic mayonnaise plus a Greek brandy or ouzo for 2,500.

Restaurant Perfetto
(R)S

> This is a pizza place in the precinct next to the Atlantic City billiards/games bar, but the pizzas are cooked in the proper Italian way in a wood oven. There's a good variety of toppings, with prices ranging from 1,100–1,500 drachmas.

> There are two tavernas on the beach, which also have a bit more of a local atmosphere than the fast food places, and reasonable food at OK prices.

Coralli taverna
(R)S

> As well as toast (which, incidentally usually means a toasted cheese and ham sandwich), omelettes and cocktails, this taverna advertises a 'Greek kitchen'. This seems to translate into the usual selection of tzatziki, taramosalata, souvlaki, moussaka and the like, rather than anything more exciting, but it's all right.

Psarotaverna
(R)S

> No name that I could discover, but it's right next door on the beach. Fish is the best bet here – ask what they have and remember that larger fish are sold by weight. Smaller fish – such as gopes or millini are more economical, and the baby squid, or kalamarakia, were good. The tomato salad had too little oil for my taste – perhaps in recognition of holidaymakers' preferences – but more was cheerfully brought on request. Chips were especially golden, crisp and hot, and being devoured enthusiastically by the Greek families enjoying fishy feasts at the other tables.
>
> Several popular hotels are clustered round a mini-suburb of Kallithea – a small development with shops, bars and a few cafés about 2 km further along the main road from the village proper. In this area, it's not unusual to meet holidaymakers who rarely, if ever, leave their hotel complexes, because everything they want in terms of facilities, shopping and entertainment is available on site. Many of the hotels are geared up to the tastes of British holidaymakers, and there are never any language problems. If that's what you're looking for, it's all very well done, but you don't get much – if any – of the flavour of Greece.

Makedonia Sun
(H)M

> Set a little way above and back from the main road, the hotel consists of a collection of two-storey white buildings with red-tiled roofs among extensive gardens. One of the hotels which is a mini-resort in itself, with its own pub, café, fast food bar, taverna, car rental office and disco. It also runs karaoke evenings – you either love them or hate them! Getting to the beach does mean leaving the hotel grounds – it's about 15 minutes' walk to the beach, across the coast road.

Athos Palace
(H)L

> Athos Palace is a very large, four-star hotel with over 1,000 beds. The main hotel building is a rather ugly white block which looks a lot better from the inside. The gardens and the view from the rooms are stunning, whether over sea or mountains, with masses of trees and flowers everywhere. Paths through the garden lead down to a long, white sandy

beach, where there's a full range of watersports. One word of warning though – don't depend on this at the beginning of the season, as the equipment may not all be available until around mid-May. Experienced divers may like to know that there's a diving school in the hotel. With six tennis courts, horse riding (lessons available), minigolf and a gym, there's plenty to keep you occupied during the day, while at night, the indoor pool area turns into a tropical bar (with the inevitable unintentional dips as a result). There are also a nightclub with Greek dancing nights, cinema and card room, so you don't need to venture out in the evenings either. The à la carte taverna is rather good, although a bit quiet and lacking in atmosphere outside the high season, with excellent fish and seafood, and a nice line in crêpes Suzette prepared at the table. Guests who prefer to have their evening meal there rather than in the main dining-room can get discount vouchers, but otherwise, a three course meal for two with a moderate wine is around 7,000 drachmas.

While the service is efficient and rather more formal than you often find in Greece, some of the staff seem to shed their serious manner with their working uniform, and chat happily to guests in the bar or night club later on. The head waiter was even spotted dancing rather idiosyncratically with a guest in the nightclub, much to the delight of his underlings!

Anyone who wants to explore beyond the hotel boundaries has plenty of options. There are bikes for hire at the hotel entrance, where you'll also usually find taxis waiting for customers. There's a bus stop immediately outside the entrance, and you can easily walk to Kriopigi (along the beach) or Kallithea village through the woods and fields behind the hotel.

Villa Princess
(H)M

A small hotel and bungalow complex right next door to the Athos Palace whose facilities are open to the guests.

Hotel Pallini
(H)L

On the other side of the Athos Palace, again with an arrangement which lets guests use the facilities of both hotels. The large, four-star Pallini has nearly 1,000 beds, and it's not a pretty sight from the outside, being a large concrete oblong with rooms in geometrically aligned rows, but quite comfortable inside. It has a mini-shopping arcade, quite a nice indoor pool with a domed glass roof, plus a nightclub and

Greek beach taverna. The gardens are lovely, however, and lead down to the beach where you'll find all the watersports you could want, including a scuba diving centre.

Map D2 **KRIOPIGI**

A small village, with most of its shops, tavernas and bars strung out along a short stretch of the main road, but with a lovely beach some 20 minutes' walk downhill along the pine-shaded side road. Watch out for flocks of sheep being herded along the beach as a short cut from one pasture to another. With some good hotels and a few tavernas – one of which offers a more interesting menu than most, Kriopigi grows on you after a while. Although

One of the many tiny shrines you'll see in roadsides everywhere.

it's gradually becoming more commercialised, it's not as slick and sophisticated as many of Kassandra's resorts and the local people are genuinely friendly and helpful.

Zacharoplasteio
(R)S

In the middle of the row of shops and tavernas on the left-hand side of the road going south, you'll find a coffee and cake place with tables in front and a lovely patio balcony at the back. Here you can sit and sip your coffee looking out over the woods and fields to the sea with hardly a person in sight. Next door is one of the many half-completed houses you find all over the area, and we were amused to see what were presumably the owners, sitting peacefully on the balcony in their folding chairs, drinks at hand, for all the world as if their house were not a mere shell behind them. In theory, the café offers bugatsa, but in September we had to content ourselves with kadaifia instead as the requisite technology had broken down and was too expensive to repair for the time being. This was no great hardship, however, as the cakes were delicious and the patio seemed like a world apart, with no sound but the insects and a cock crowing somewhere nearby.

Christos' Taverna
(R)M

On the left-hand side of the road going south, on the corner of the road leading down to the beach. From the outside the taverna looks pretty ordinary, and the view of the main road is not particularly attractive, but the new wooden balustrade and its covering of creeper is gradually concealing more and more of the outside world from view. In any case, the menu – promising 'tasty food from mammy's kitchen' – makes it worth a visit. Each day, the owner's mother cooks special 'dishes of the day'. Sometimes they're written up on a blackboard, otherwise Christos will explain the day's offerings to you, and is genuinely concerned that you choose something you'll enjoy. When I asked for a dish described as 'Christos' clay pot', he told me that it was rather unusual, and was I sure I wanted it? He had eaten it when visiting Bulgaria, and it consists of spicy sausages, tomatoes, mushrooms, olives, green peppers, feta and soft eggs – all baked together in the clay pot and topped with bubbling browned cheese. It sounds a bit strange, but actually it was really delicious. Served with a very good tomato and olive salad, plus a beer, the meal was very good value at 1,500 drachmas. Other 'specials' included stuffed courgettes, moussaka and chicken cooked with onions, and the selection of salads included some unusual combinations like beetroot and peppers. It's the sort of place where customers soon turn into 'regulars', and I noticed one afternoon that a group of British holidaymakers had their tea, beer and snacks delivered as soon as they sat down – obviously an arrangement that had arisen naturally after previous visits and was very satisfactory all round.

Taverna Nikos
(R)S

On the right-hand side of the main road coming from the north, Taverna Nikos is owned and run by a friendly individual called Yannis rather than Nikos! His English wife Jill runs the clothes shop opposite, and the atmosphere in the taverna is very relaxed and friendly. The food's not bad either. The swordfish steak is particularly good – large and juicy, without any trace of the dryness which can be a problem with this rather meaty fish. It was seasoned with flat parsley and lemons and grilled to a turn. This is also a good place to sample pasticcio, the real Greek pasta dish made with layers of fat macaroni, minced meat and tomato sauce and topped with a light cheese sauce. The starters and salads are good, although not particularly special, and the prices reasonable. Expect to pay around 6,000 drachmas for two including a bottle of medium quality wine.

Zorba's Taverna
(R)S

On the opposite side of the road, it's the last taverna you come to going south. Screened from the road with greenery and lit with small lamps, it looks quite attractive at night, although the decor inside is not all that smart. Nevertheless, it's comfortable and easy-going, and the staff seemed very good at watching the football match on TV with their neighbours while simultaneously keeping an eye open for customers needing their attention! The menu has something to suit most tastes, without being ambitious – souvlakia, various meats in sauces, swordfish steaks and the usual salads, plus a good selection of locally caught fish. The 'lavraki' – firm white-fleshed fish grilled with lemon and flat parsley were good, and the aubergines were simply fried in oil rather than frittered, but fresh and hot, like the chips. Local red wine, served in a jug, was not for the discerning palate, but quite drinkable. Expect to pay around 6,000 drachmas for two, with local wine.

Hotel Kassandra Palace
(H)L

A large four-star hotel midway between the villages of Kriopigi and Polihrono. The low-rise buildings cover only a tiny proportion of the surrounding land, which is laid out as a beautiful garden, with exotic flowers, lawns, trees and vines leading down to the sandy beach. There are 400 olive trees too, which produce a tonne of olives and two tonnes of olive oil every year. The fat, juicy black olives, which are served in the hotel restaurants, are among the best I've ever tasted. Despite the size, the hotel isn't at all impersonal, and the staff are especially friendly and helpful. With a choice of bars, and an excellent à la carte taverna and comfortable indoor and outdoor lounge areas and riding and watersports facilities close at hand, the hotel offers the perfect holiday environment. You do have to make a bit of an effort to drag yourself away to see something of the surrounding area, but there is a free bus service to Kriopigi several times a day and the reception staff will happily call a taxi for you if there isn't one waiting at the gate. Although my personal preference is usually for smaller, more atmospheric hotels, I liked the Kassandra Palace very much, and the gardens give it a real feeling of space and peace.

Kassandra Bay Hotel
(H)M

A small but very comfortable family-run hotel set into the hillside near the village of Kriopigi. It's a low, three-storey building about a 25-minute walk from the Kriopigi beach, among the sweet-smelling pine woods – and if you can't face the uphill walk back, there's always the option of using the hotel's courtesy bus. It's a similar walk to the smallish village of Kriopigi, where you'll find shops, bars and tavernas. While it doesn't have all the facilities offered by the larger hotels, it does have a poolside bar, restaurant, indoor bar and terrace, it's in a very attractive spot and quiet and friendly. A good choice for those who prefer to be a little off the beaten track.

Hotel Alexander the Great
(H)M

A three-star family-run hotel set among trees a little way above the beach 1 km outside Kriopigi. You can either walk the 80 m down to the beach, or take the lift. The red-roofed buildings are covered in a green creeper and decorated in Macedonian style, and there's an open-air taverna, café and beach grill, plus a tennis court, massage room and a choice of watersports.

Theo Bungalows
(H)M

A pretty little complex of low white buildings set on a hill among the trees in pretty gardens. There's a pool and small restaurant, but it's a fair walk down to the beach (800 m) and a bit less to the village of Kriopigi. The accommodation is simple and comfortable, and this would be a good choice if you want somewhere quiet and peaceful without too much going on.

Hotel Kriopigi
(H)M

A comfortable hotel on the outskirts of the village, built in Macedonian style around the swimming pool. There's a taverna on the roof with great views and an à la carte menu. It's a good 20-minute walk down to the beach, although there is a shuttle bus from the village which might be useful coming back.

Map D3 **POLIHRONO**

If you're looking for sun, sea and sand, Polihrono is ideal, but it doesn't have a great deal of atmosphere or individuality. Behind the long beach is a row of the usual souvenir shops, bars, mini-markets and the like, and several tavernas where English breakfast is prominently advertised.

Heraclis Taverna
(R)S

Quite a fun place with a jolly atmosphere and a reasonably interesting menu with half an eye directed at their German clientele. Goulash soup, for instance, is hardly a Greek dish, but there's also bean soup and even pea soup which tasted like a thinner version of our own pea and ham soup! There's a good selection of fish, and interestingly, we were informed that blacktail and red snapper were not available in September 'because now the fish make babies!' Something to think about when you're swimming! The kalamaria (squid) were good, while the plate of mixed fried fish was excellent value at 1,500 drachmas – and could easily have been shared by two people.

Russian salad can be a bit bland, but here the mixed vegetables were dressed in a good mayonnaise – again a large portion for 450 drachmas. Green beans in a tomato sauce seemed popular with other customers, but you could also have pizza, pasta or even sausage and chips. For around 5,000 drachmas, you get a substantial meal for two with beer or soft drinks – but unless you're very hungry, it might be worth ordering fewer dishes than usual as the servings are generous.

Hotel Neapolis
(H)S

A small hotel right on the beach and a short walk from the rows of shops and bars along the front. It's simple, but rather attractive with a pizzeria and bar and a fridge in your room; and pretty balconies looking directly on to the sea.

Hotel Odysseas
(H)S

A relatively small (56-bed) family-run hotel a couple of minutes' walk from the beach and the resort centre. Simple but quite comfortable, there's a pretty little garden bar, but nothing much else in the way of facilities. A convenient base if you want to explore Polihrono and the surrounding area.

Sun Hotel
(H)S

Another small and friendly hotel close to the beach and the resort facilities. Simple and relatively quiet, with a little courtyard garden but no other public facilities.

Map D3 **HANIOTI**

This is one of the larger and more sophisticated resorts on this coast, and very popular with Greek people, especially the young, as well as with foreign tourists. The beach is long and clean, but gets very crowded in parts, with sunbeds and umbrellas crammed cheek by jowl. There are all kinds of facilities for watersports, plus a couple of beach bars where you can get a drink and a snack. In the evenings, the centre of activities moves to the area around the square, where there are lots of jewellery and 'Greek art' shops plus a few clothes boutiques. Many of the tavernas try to cater for what they think is the foreigners' tastes, while some helpfully advertise 'set

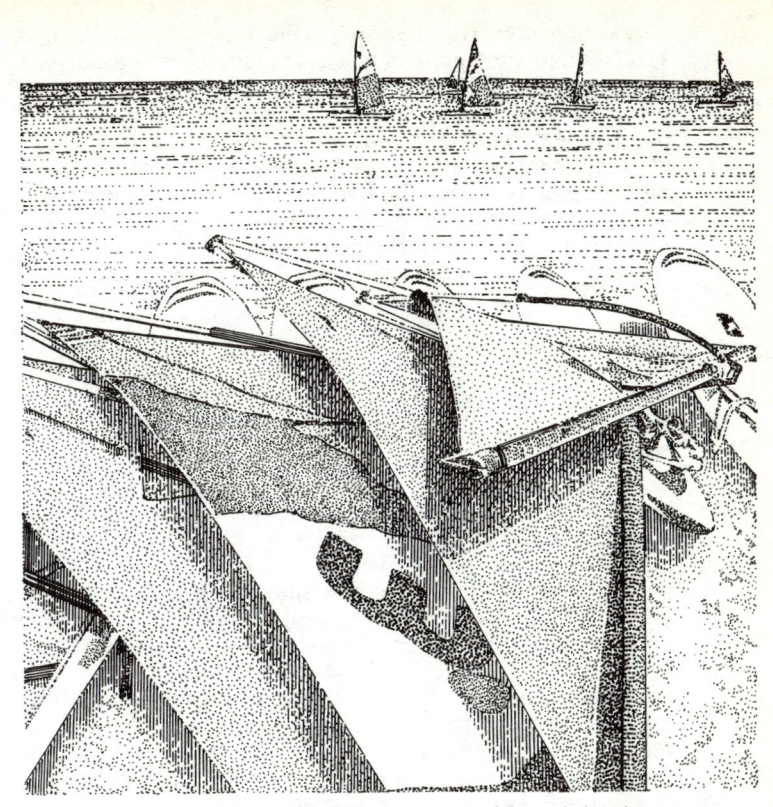

You'll find windsurfing schools on many of the main beaches.

menus' in the French style. The choices are a bit unexciting, but usually good value. With several music bars popular with younger people, the area can be noisy late at night, so if you're staying somewhere near the centre, ear plugs could be worth packing if you're not a night owl. Although it's unashamedly commercial, I found myself liking Hanioti much more than I expected, possibly because its popularity with Greek holidaymakers prevents it from turning into one of those anonymous Euro-Med resorts which could be anywhere.

Dionysos Taverna
(R)M

Just off the bottom left-hand corner of the square isn't one of the cheaper options but the food is good and the atmosphere very welcoming. The charming waiters, fluent in both English and German, are happy to discuss the menu, and especially to explain all about the various fish on offer. Lavraki – 'white meat, not many bones' – was simply grilled and dressed with thin lemon and coriander sauce and utterly delicious. The menu here makes a good effort at describing some of the dishes on offer: htipiti, the feta cheese concoction with whole black peppers, for example, is called 'spicy cheese dip', which sums it up perfectly. Fresh fish for two, plus three salads and a bottle of Robola – a dry white wine from the Ionian island of Cephalonia – came to 7,700 drachmas.

Ouzeri/taverna
(R)S

Without any obvious name, but next door to the Thomson/Doucas Tours office round the corner from the Kiss Bar. It has a real Greek look about it, with flowers and little lamps and a dozen or so tables. The whole experience was completely unforgettable from start to finish. For a start, the young waiter presented us with a menu, then read carefully and slowly from a piece of paper: 'I do not speak English. Please look at menu and show me', then smiled triumphantly at having successfully negotiated the first hurdle of the evening. More were to come, however. The said menu provided a few cheap laughs, offering such dishes as fried squit, a lot of kind fishes and stakes, but once we got over that, the choice looked interesting and attractive. Unfortunately, our decision to go for a meze-style meal of various salads and starters was foiled by the fact that the first few dishes we ordered were off. Trying to order in Greek just seemed to confuse the poor young man still further, so pointing was the only option. Eventually we managed to light on various things that weren't off – and it was well worth the effort. The 'garlic rissole/grill' tasted more of rigani – the Greek version of oregano – than garlic and were utterly delicious. Village sausages turned out to be two enormous spicy and garlicky sausages full of real meat and both main dishes came with potatoes, peas and grilled tomatoes. The tomato salad was likewise enormous and garnished with sprigs of feathery fresh dill. The red wine, again ordered in Greek to avoid confusion, turned out to be rosé, although the young man asserted it was red when questioned. We decided that he couldn't face explaining that red wine was off too, so we gave in graciously, and allowed him to wrap it carefully in a napkin and place it in the ice bucket beside the table. The food was good, freshly cooked and imaginatively presented, and the entertainment consisted of watching other customers go through much the same performance when they sat down. You either find this kind of thing funny or hate it, and at least two tables' worth of would-be diners gave up in despair and went elsewhere to eat. Those of us who remained thoroughly enjoyed the whole thing, and our sense of solidarity at having surmounted all the difficulties was obviously shared by the waiter, who rewarded those who stayed the course with a complimentary glass of tsipouro at the end of our meals. I should point out that someone who'd eaten there previously told us that this state of chaos wasn't normal – the owner who was normally in charge speaks reasonable English, and so many dishes were off because it was relatively late in the season. Even without the cabaret, however, it's worth going for the food and good value at about 3,500 drachmas for two.

Summertime Taverna
(R)M

Widely advertised with its own street signs, Summertime Taverna promises excellent Greek and international cooking. The general decor and style is a bit upmarket of your average taverna, and superclean with crisp linen napkins and cloths, and fast efficient service. The menu was actually a bit too international for my tastes, majoring on steaks and including what they call, rather imaginatively I thought, Château Brian (5,500 for two). It's about 1,000 drachmas more per head than most of the other tavernas, but steak lovers assured me the quality was excellent and well worth the money.

Taverna Avra
(R)S

Taverna Avla on the main square is one of those offering set-price menus as well as the usual à la carte selection. For example, canneloni or souvlaki or pork steak, Greek salad, dessert and a glass of wine: 2,400 drachmas; soup, fish special, Greek salad, a glass of beer or wine and dessert 2,100 and pepper steak plus Greek salad and the rest 2,500. I opted for what the menu described as fried shrimps, which turned out to be seven giant Mediterranean prawns cooked in a light coating and served with lemons, for 1,950 drachmas. The place lacked atmosphere, but its vantage point overlooking the central square meant you could enjoy watching all the comings and goings, although it might be rather noisy on busy evenings.

Café Eclair
(R)S

Café Eclair on the main square is a good place for coffee and pastries during the day or to finish your evening after dinner. During the day, you can get warm bugatsa with either cream or cheese, and they still serve it in the evening – cold but still very good. The waiter is something of a joker, and one evening decorated a willing Greek woman's rather elaborate coiffure like a cocktail – complete with paper umbrellas, straws and finally sparklers – which he actually lit. He also demonstrated how to pour out coffee from a Greek pot without it going all over the table – a trick I'd never managed to master before. The café has a good mix of Greek and foreign customers, and a relaxed friendly atmosphere.

Hotel Strand
(H)M

In a lovely situation right on the beach, this comfortable unpretentious hotel shares facilities with its bigger sister next door, the Hotel Grand. There's a small garden area around the pool (with its own whirlpool), and right next to it a bar-cum-taverna with shady tables overlooking the beach which is particularly attractive in the evenings. The village centre is only a few minutes' walk away, but far enough for the hotel itself to be relatively quiet and with a certain amount of real Greek atmosphere.

Dionysos Hotel
(H)S

A combination of hotel and apartments – the latter have a small kitchenette with a fridge – that's about 500 m away from the resort centre and the beach. Clean and quite comfortable, the hotel has a pool, à la carte restaurant and a bar and is set in a pretty garden. Relaxed and informal, it would make a good base for exploring Hanioti and the surrounding area.

Sousouras Hotel
(H)M

Sousouras Hotel is in an idyllic location in lovely gardens and right on the beach at the edge of the resort. It's a combination of hotel and apartments, spread around a collection of small bungalows that blend acceptably into the background. Facilities include a snack bar, boutique, three bars, a souvenir shop, children's play area – and there's live music in the taverna some evenings. You're far enough from the centre here (about 300 m) to be away from the hubbub of the evenings and early hours!

Hotel Sarantis
(H)S

A small, family-run hotel on the outskirts of the resort among the pine trees. The apartments have a small kitchenette, and there's a bar and a small pool, but for other facilities you have to take a short walk into the centre. Friendly and comfortable, about 400 m from the beach.

Hotel Hanioti
(H)S

Not for the early-to-bed holidaymakers, this small and very friendly hotel is close to the resort centre and the nightlife.

Hotel Hanioti Village
(H)S

Situated on the outskirts of the resort, just off the main coastal road which you have to cross to reach the beach. A simple hotel consisting of several low-rise buildings in well-kept gardens with its own pool and a bar-cum-snack bar.

Hotel Plaza
(H)S

A small (32-bed) and relatively simple hotel close to the beach and the central square, with a bar that can sometimes get pretty lively into the early hours. Plenty of atmosphere.

Hilltop Hotel
(H)M

A very nice Macedonian-style building set among pine woods and olive trees with stunning views over the sea. It's a very comfortable family-run hotel in an attractive hillside site, with its own pool, bar and restaurant. The 10-minute walk down to the beach and the centre of Hanioti is no problem, but of course you then have to walk back up! Worth it, though, if only for the view!

Olympic Kosmas Hotel
(H)M

> Comfortable, if not madly atmospheric, this complex of room and studios is built around a pool in a peaceful spot on the outskirts of Hanioti. With its own attractive poolside restaurant and bar, it's not too far from the beach, and it's relaxed and informal.

Map D3 **PEFKOHORI**

> Although there's nothing very distinctive about Pefkohori, I think it is one of the more attractive resorts on the Kassandra peninsula. Basically, it's just a long, white sand and shingle beach with a newly tiled promenade behind lined with shops, bars and tavernas, but it has a friendly, welcoming feel about it. Part of its charm is that it's not too big or over-commercialised, and the local people seem genuinely pleased to meet and talk to the visitors. There are newly planted trees and flower beds all along the prom and very pretty street lamps. Several of the cafés along the front advertise breakfast, and there are a couple of ice cream places too, plus the usual collection of supermarket, souvenir and beach shops. Wherever you choose to sit, whether to eat or drink, you have a great view out to sea towards Sithonia, with the so-called Turtle Island ahead of you. As you'll see, it's named for its shape, not its wildlife. At the moment, Pefkohori is relatively quiet, but there's a new villa complex with pool near the middle of the village, and what looks like another one under construction among the pine woods at the far end of the beach, so it may well get busier over the next few years.

Taverna Toroneos
(R)M

> The sign offers the irresistible promise 'Everything fish you want grilled', and they really do try harder with the menu. The pleasant young waiter recommended the fried pumpkin rather than the fried red peppers I had asked for with tzatziki, explaining that that particular combination was considered more tasty in Greece. It was certainly very good, but the grilled squid stuffed with soft feta and fresh coriander and served in lemon sauce was one of the nicest taverna dishes I sampled. It always seems to me that you can tell a lot about a taverna by the bread it serves. It's hardly ever less than good and always

fresh, but occasionally you come across something a bit different – which shows that someone is taking a little extra trouble. Here, the bread had a yellowish colour with a good flavour, and was very crumbly – I was told it was a speciality of the local baker. With a beer, this very good lunch for one came to 2,600 drachmas.

Zum Georg
(R)M

Zum Georg apparently translates as George's Place and is about halfway along the front. You need a strong will not to try this one if you're walking by because there are usually two very persuasive old men sitting on the outside tables to lure you in. One speaks excellent English, the other German, so they can cater for all likely eventualities between them. Unless you're determined to go elsewhere, you might as well give in, then you can enjoy the cabaret as other passers by are subjected to the same treatment. High pressure it isn't, but rather conducted in a jokey spirit – and may even extend to the offer of a prawn or some other titbit from their lunch to taste as the final clincher. Once inside, you're likely to be invited into the kitchen to choose your meal, which I actually find more difficult than picking from the menu, because it all looks good. The fish and salads are fine, especially the unusual grated carrot salad, and the whole grilled prawns looked appealing too, but if you feel like a change, the meatballs in tomato sauce are tasty and good value at 950 drachmas. A dish which I hadn't seen elsewhere – kalamaria stifado – is squid stewed in a clay pot with tomatoes and onions and was utterly delicious. The crayfish starter, strongly flavoured with dill was exceptionally good too. Horta – variously translated as greens, country vegetable, village cabbage – was actually rather disappointing, something like cold pickled spinach leaves. We were told elsewhere, however, that this is primarily a winter or spring dish, when the young greens are picked after the rains, so perhaps this was the reason. A fairly gluttonous meal for two with beer or soft drinks would cost around 4,500 drachmas.

Hotel Kopsis
(H)S

Small and simple, with no claims to luxury, this is nevertheless a rather charming hotel right on the beach about 1.5 km from the centre of Pefkohori. It's set among pine trees in its own small garden, and has a nice, family atmosphere with a real Greek feeling.

Hotel Zeus
(H)M

> Right on the seafront, this little hotel has a friendly feeling with comfortable rooms, all with balconies overlooking the sea. It's an attractive traditional-style building, and a good choice if you want something more than basic accommodation without sacrificing a local atmosphere.

Ioli Village Apartments
(H)S

> A new development of three-storey white apartment blocks with wooden balconies, set in pretty gardens around a pool. It's self-catering, with a basic kitchenette in each apartment. There are two bars, and it's only a short walk into the centre of the village to buy supplies or sample the taverna fare. The beach is about 500 m from the complex through an underpass and the bus runs through the village.

Map D3   **PALIOURI**

> This inland village is virtually on the tip of the peninsula, and the views down through the trees to the sea on both sides are absolutely stunning. The village itself is a maze of steep narrow streets lined with nineteenth-century houses. In the centre you come across the church to one side of a very attractive square with an old-fashioned 'kafeneion' much favoured by elderly gentlemen arguing and playing backgammon. I was quite excited to see a shop claiming to specialise in cheese, but instead of the unusual Greek varieties I'd hoped to find, there were Cheddar, Danish blue and others all too familiar from my local supermarket. There's also a promising-looking shop called Summertime Memories – but in September it had a rather abandoned look, so I never discovered just what it sold. Opposite the church, behind a low red and white brick wall, is Lemoniades taverna, with a simple menu consisting mostly of fish and the usual starters and salads.

Map D3   **CHROUSSO**

> The beach (follow the sign to the Chrousso Village Apartments) is a semi-circular bay of white sand backed by pine-covered

hills and absolutely beautiful. The sea is like a mill pond, and so clear you can see your shadow on the bottom when you're swimming. At one end there's a small jetty which is the starting point for boat trips to see the monasteries of Athos, but the excursions have to be booked in advance and you can't buy tickets on the spot. There's nothing much on the beach other than a bar which is a replica of a wooden boat, covered in thatch, and sunk into the sand. It looks nice, but it's not actually very practical and the music is too loud for my taste.

Some 10 minutes' walk back along a tree-shaded path there's a little supermarket, just outside the entrance to the Chrousso Village Apartments.

Chrousso Village Apartments
(H)M

A relatively new development of 86 apartments, set in well-tended gardens around a pool. It's an attractive and well-designed development – small blocks of three-storey white buildings with red-tiled roofs and wooden balconies – that merges quite discreetly into the wooden countryside, comfortable and friendly. There's a poolside bar and an à la carte taverna, and plenty of facilities, including a tennis court and boutique. It's a lovely spot, but very quiet and rather isolated, so you'd need transport if you want to get out and about. If it's not too hot, you can walk the 2 km to Paliouri or the 7 km to Pefkohori, where you can get the bus, but there's nothing else within reasonable reach.

Map D3 **LOUTRA**

A small village with no real sandy beach, but little pebble and rock enclaves where you can sunbathe or swim in the clear water. Climbing up the road out of the village, there's a taverna and bar in a beautiful spot high above the sea.

Taverna Villa Stella
(R)S

Tables inside a large room with huge windows on three sides looking out to sea. Although the sign says it's open all day, there was little sign of life when I was there in September, so I can't report on the food, but even if it's nothing special, the position would make it worth a visit. Similarly, there's a bar next door which has seats ranged down a series of terraces

Kassandra peninsula

The rocky shore at Loutra.

among the trees and overlooking the sea, but this was definitely closed for the season in September.

| Map D3 | **NEA SKIONI** |

This is a real fishing village, with working boats in the little harbour and a definite whiff of fish in the air. All around you see men sat in gardens or on flowery patios mending nets, or talking to their neighbours and watching the world go by in the traditional kafeneions (coffee houses) on the narrow main street. There are a couple of tavernas along this street too, mainly aimed at tourists from Germany and with menus and signs in German rather than English, offering gyros (doner kebab) and pizza rather than anything more interesting. There's a long sandy beach but nothing in the way of sunbeds or umbrellas, and a taverna and bar just behind the jetty.

Taverna Akrogiali
R)S

A pretty-looking place, with flowers in a raised concrete bed along the front and climbing roses around the edges. Fresh fish is, as might be expected, plentiful and not too expensive, and the salads are fine, but I didn't find it the friendliest of places and the loo was somewhat unwholesome!

Next door, the bar Scala is a pretty spot to sit and take in the view if you just want a drink or a coffee.

Leaving the village on the main road going north, you'll see a taverna on your right.

Taverna Elias
R)S

Taverna Elias, with an old fishing boat called 'Green peace' in its parking area, has tables spread in a garden amid olive trees overlooking the sea. A good selection of fish and other seafood, plus meatballs, fillet and grilled chicken, freshly cooked and reasonably priced – about 4,500 for two with beer or soft drinks.

Map D2 **POSSIDI**

Along the little promontory around the fishing village of Possidi, you'll find miles of relatively empty beaches where you can get away from it all. The village itself is very small – no more than a strip of buildings along the sea, with several recently built low-rise apartment developments and a couple of hotels. There's a rather good supermarket with newspapers, magazines, fruit and plenty of picnic supplies, and a couple of simple tavernas with quite good, inexpensive food. The hotels are attractive in their different ways – but at the moment, they are almost exclusively occupied by clients of German tour operators and not offered by British companies.

Taverna
R)S

This taverna without any advertised name is at the far end of the beach road past the supermarket on the left. Hidden away behind the flowering plants and grapevines are about a dozen tables in a quiet and peaceful setting overlooking the beach. The furniture is a little ramshackle, but the atmosphere is nice, with villagers sitting around having a drink and chatting while other customers eat. Along one side there are a couple of tables under a vine-covered trellis, which in September is groaning with great bunches of grapes. I sat there one evening watching three young men cutting them down and flinging them into a small, polythene-lined cart, laughing and singing as they worked. The menu offers a good choice – the usual starters and salads, pasticcio (900 drachmas), red mullet (10,000 per kilo) and other fish ranging from 4–9,000 a kilo, moussaka, chops and burgers all at around 1,000 drachmas. Souvlaki moskou was lovely – tiny pieces of pork grilled on wooden skewers and flavoured with lemon and rigani. The salads were plentiful and fresh, with some of the reddest tomatoes I've ever seen and the meal, including half a bottle of white wine was excellent value at 2,500 drachmas.

There are also a couple of bars and snack bars if you just want a drink or something light, plus a fish taverna right on the beach – although this did seem to have rather unpredictable opening hours, so shouldn't be relied on by the hungry.

Hotel Possidi Holidays
(H)L

A beautifully designed complex set into the pine-covered hillside and overlooking the long sandy beach. Many of the rooms are in bungalows above the main building, and all have balconies and air conditioning. As well as a pool and a taverna there are excellent sports facilities, plus a restaurant and mini-market.

Map D2   **KALANDRA**

This inland village is a nice place to stop for a coffee and a wander about – you can see most of it in about 10 minutes. It has some attractive old buildings and lovely views up into the countryside and pine woods and down over the sea. On the right as you come up into the village there are jewellery workshops (or 'atelier' as the sign has it) where you can see the goldsmith at work, and buy if you want. Just round to the left, past the supermarket is the Plato coffee bar, where you can watch the comings and goings in the small central square, or, like some holidaymakers I met, wait for the pharmacy next door to open. It seems to be the only one in the area, but unfortunately, the owner is prone to 'go for walks sometimes', so its opening hours are unpredictable. There is a cake shop too, and a couple of snack-type tavernas, with nothing much to offer besides souvlakia and pizza.

Map D2 **SKALA FOURKAS**

In the centre of this small-to-middle sized, fairly commercial resort is a large open square with a supermarket, souvenir shops and plenty of tavernas ranged round the edges. A paved walkway leads off from one corner by the supermarket, past the Thomson office, a bureau de change which is open all hours, and a couple of souvenir/beach shops into a long development of fairly new low-rise apartments. Behind the buildings on the furthest side of the square lies the beach of rough sand stretching a long way in both directions. It's not very wide, and for some distance is covered with sunbeds and beach umbrellas packed shoulder to shoulder. There are watersports galore, most of which are considerably cheaper here than in other parts of Halkidiki. What's more, if you care to walk a bit further in either direction, there are long stretches of much more sparsely populated strand, with even the occasional tree to give some shade. There are only a couple of tavernas right on the beach (see below), but there are one or two bars where you can get drinks and snacks.

While Skala Fourkas (or Fourka Beach as some of the brochures have it) certainly isn't a traditional village, and is hardly peaceful, being very popular with both British and German tourists, it is a relaxed friendly place and not unbearably noisy. Except, that is, for the dogs. All day you see them lying in the shade and sleeping peacefully, but at night they wake up and bark as though their lives depended on it. Presumably they're strays, although none look particularly hungry or mangy, but people staying in apartments at the back of the resort told me they'd been reduced to chucking small rocks from their balconies in the early hours to try and stop the din.

The presence of so many apartments means that there are plenty of tavernas to meet the demand, and some make a deliberate effort to satisfy what they think are north-European tastes – not always successfully in my view. However, it's well meant, and illustrates the friendliness and willingness to please of the local people.

Taki's fish taverna
(R)S

One of two tavernas next to each other right on the beach. This one was very popular with Greek customers, and is very attractive, with blue painted wood and rush chairs, and about twelve tables ranged along a wooden platform outside and more inside the glass doors. It's lovely to look straight out to sea, and one evening, there was a fishing boat pulled up on to the sand, with several fishermen mending their nets by moonlight and chatting to passing friends and neighbours. The menu features several 'home-made dishes of the day', including moussaka, pasticcio and swordfish in tomato and garlic sauce. There's a big choice of locally caught fish, including the intriguingly named 'murmuring fish', and this was one of the few tavernas I came across which gave sample prices for individual portions. This was a little confusing in practice, because while it said that the normal price was 9,000 drachmas per kilo, the special offer price was 5,500 while an individual portion of red mullet, for example, was given as 1,200 drachmas, presumably calculated on the basis of the special offer. In any case, the fish looked wonderful as I watched neighbouring Greek families share out large specimens of a bream-like fish, grilled, garnished with flat parsley and served with lemons and a thin lemony sauce. The swordfish 'dish of the day' was very good too – with lots of tasty sauce, parsley and whole cloves of garlic (1,500 drachmas). Pikantiki was a salad I hadn't tried before, and consisted of grated white cabbage and carrots in a lemon and oil dressing – not unlike coleslaw without the mayonnaise. The five-year-old house wine sounded interesting but was a mistake! Served in a frosted glass jug, it was a queer peachy colour with a funny tang to it – rather like a sharp white wine with a spot of cooking sherry added. Nothing much lost, however, as it was only 600 drachmas for half a litre.

Taverna Pitza Asterix
(R)S

On the left-hand side of the road, just behind the beach fish tavernas and the souvenir shop. A quiet little place that turned out to be much nicer than I'd expected from its name, which conjured up images of fast food and loud music. The little terrace is shaded by trees and lots of flowering geraniums, and the charming lady in charge was helpful and as friendly as our limited knowledge of each other's languages allowed. The menu did indeed have pizza and lots of pasta, but there was also a good choice of Greek dishes, including stuffed kalamaria filled with soft feta and parsley bearing no resemblance to the chewy rings fried in batter which put so many people off squid. The salads were nice too, and there was German-style beer on draught, as well as Amstel and a selection of wine. In fact, even if you didn't want to eat, it's a pleasant spot to while away the odd afternoon hour with a drink, and not expensive. Around 2,000 for a main course, a couple of salads and a beer.

Zorba's Restaurant
(R)S

Another relatively quiet place on the main square with a rather traditional ambience: blue painted wooden furniture, a plain wooden roof and no loud pop music, or in fact music of any kind, a considerable rarity. An appealing selection of hot and cold starters and salads, including red peppers, fried aubergines and courgettes (all at around 400 drachmas), plus grilled octopus at 1,000. Main courses ranged from chicken, liver and moussaka (900 each) to pork or lamb chops (1,200) and steak at 2,000 drachmas. This is a good place to find out how fried kalamaria should taste – light and crisp and melt-in-the-mouth. Good value too – a main course, fresh golden chips, Greek salad and beer for 2,300 drachmas.

Taverna Faros
(R)M

This taverna in the central square area is quite large but seemed to have no trouble at all filling its many outdoor tables. A bit bright and crammed for my liking, but the menu is varied and inexpensive, and the service cheerful and friendly. It is popular with families, perhaps because there is a special children's menu – and the fish fingers and chips, plus tomato ketchup in a red squeezy bottle, were produced with many smiles and flourishes. The menu is in English, a strange mixture of genuine Greek cuisine, such as fried feta cheese, fried mussels or mussels in spicy tomato sauce, and the less exotic, including jacket potatoes, roast beef, omelettes and fish and chips. Many main dishes come with a few chips and token vegetables, but whatever your preference, you'd be sure to find something that appealed from the enormous choice on offer. The price of a meal depends very much on what you choose, but it is not an expensive place.

Mama's
(R)S

> Just off the main square along the street leading back up to the main road, Mama's is middle-sized, with wooden chairs, geraniums and a grapevine growing over the awning to conceal the not very interesting view. This was a place that tried very hard but didn't quite get it right as far as I was concerned. The staff speak good English and are friendly and helpful, and the menu looks interesting enough: lamb or pork in wine sauce, kleftiko, stuffed aubergine and fish soup for instance. The first surprise came when I'd ordered fried aubergines, tomato and cucumber salad and chicken from the oven. I was smilingly asked if I wanted it all together. It hadn't occurred to me that it could be otherwise, but someone had obviously pointed out at some time that starters usually come first, and they were trying to please. The second surprise was when the food came. The plates of salad were huge, but that's not unusual, but the chicken was on a vast plate accompanied by great heaps of chips, rice, peas and carrots. The chicken was delicious, although the vegetables weren't, and when the waiter came to remove my half-empty plates, I told him there was too much for me. 'Everybody says same thing', he smiled sadly. There must be a lesson there somewhere. Anyway, this vast feast plus a beer came to only 2,200.

Elite
(R)M

> A zacharoplasteio or cake and coffee place on the square underneath the restaurant Bella Venezia. There's a lovely selection of cakes and pastries plus pizza and spinach pies to eat there or take away, plus loukoumades and my favourite – bugatsa. There's a pretty veranda furnished in yellow and white where you can sit with your morning coffee and cakes or after a meal and watch the world go by. I actually saw a man in a straw hat stroll casually past with two goats on leads as though it were a perfectly normal thing to do on a Sunday morning – but then perhaps it is if you live in Skala Fourkas.

Hotel Australia
(H)S

> At the far end of Fourka's long, sandy beach, nestling behind the trees, this small, simple hotel is a good base for a sun and sand holiday. It has its own restaurant and a pleasant bar under an awning right on the beach, and it's just a short walk along to the seafront to the centre of the resort.

Map D2 **SIVIRI**

The resort has a rather unfinished air, with building work suspended on various half-complete structures, and apartment blocks waiting for the next storey to be added. The beach is quite good – long, curved and sandy, but a bit weedy at one end, and backed by pine woods. There's a supermarket, plus an ouzeri, cake shop/café and several tavernas along the road behind the beach. Few of them have signs or names in English, and the waiters seem to know more German than English, so you may need to be quite inventive to communicate.

Psarotaverna Stathis
(R)S

This is the white building with the red-tiled roof and blue shutters just by the jetty, with blue wood and rush chairs and

A typical Halkidiki house with its wooden shutters and balcony.

tables on a raised platform just above the beach. The menu here is simple enough: 'Is fish. You like fish?' followed by an invitation to 'come and look'. You go to the kitchen and make your selection from what's on offer. Fridges are opened to reveal great trays of sparkling fish of all different sizes – melanouri, red mullet, 'sea beatles' or whatever is in season. I chose melanouri – smallish silver-grey fish with firm white flesh and not too bony. Two were weighed out for me before being prepared – 200 grammes! Grilled and served with parsley and lemons, they were delicious, as were the salads. The aubergine salad (melitzanosalata) had a good rough texture and sesame seeds in it, while the enormous tomato and cucumber salad came complete with onions, lots of flat parsley and chives and thin strips of pale green pepper. There must have been a pound of tomatoes at least, but all this, plus a beer, came to 2,500 drachmas.

Taverna Timotheos
(R)S

One block back from the beach, but still with a view past the fish taverna in front. A relatively ordinary menu, but the smoked mackerel was good, the service friendly and the price very reasonable. The mackerel, plus a couple of salads and a beer was only 1,600 drachmas.

There's another fish taverna towards the other end of the beach from the jetty, but although the menu looked OK, it had less atmosphere. Basically, it consisted of lots of tables under an awning in front of a half-completed building so you were effectively eating in the middle of a building site, but no doubt it will improve when (or if) the construction is finished.

There is also an ouzeri called Nikos at the back of the beach on the other side of the jetty, but I never managed to find it open!

Sithonia peninsula

The resorts along the 40-kilometre strip of coastline between Nea Moudania and Nikiti are counted as being in Sithonia, although they are not on the actual peninsula. From the main, sometimes relatively busy road, you don't get much impression of their presence, and you usually have to turn off down the individual side roads to reach the resorts themselves which are located along the sea.

Map B2	**GERAKINI**

Gerakini is a recent tourist development, with a few tavernas and shops among the trees bordering the seafront. The beach itself is fairly ordinary, with a mine at one end! The shops are the usual tourist ones, including a jeweller and a supermarket.

Olympion taverna
(R)S

Olympion taverna is at the end of the row, nearest the mine, and well shaded by palm trees. Although it's definitely not smart – no cloths on the tables – the food was surprisingly good. Lurking among the standard menu offerings are a few more interesting dishes, including htipiti – feta with whole not black peppers mixed to a texture like cottage cheese, fish soup, Greek chicken soup and something excitingly described as 'gypsy pork meat' which I have to admit I didn't investigate further! Some of the fish is quite reasonably priced, with trout for 850 drachmas, and mussels with tomato and pepper sauce 950. The fried courgettes were cooked with chopped garlic and nicer than most I tasted elsewhere. White wine in a jug is not for connoisseurs, but fine if you can live with the cheap and cheerful. Expect to pay about 3,000 drachmas for a meal with house wine.

Hotel Gerakina Beach
(H)M

A large, three-star hotel set in twenty acres of gardens behind the beach, where there's a snack bar and a selection of watersports, including a windsurfing school. The main building is low-rise – only five floors – and most of the accommodation is in one- or two-storey bungalows linked by pathways through the pretty gardens. There are masses of activities on offer, including tennis, volleyball, a pool table and fitness room, and there's even a sauna if it's not hot enough for you outside!

Map B3   PSAKOUDIA

Some five kilometres along the road, there's a sign for the beach road which leads down to the seafront and the little resort of Psakoudia. The beach is long and clean, with pedaloes and a few other water activities on offer, and a rather trendy beach bar at one end. Immediately behind the beach, there's a strip of tavernas, tourist shops and bars – including one which claims to be 'The Original London Pub'. Predictably, it's like no pub you've ever seen, in London or anywhere else, with tables under an awning where you can sit for hours with a single beer or coffee and watch the world go by – if you can stand the rather loud pop music. Tavernas favour the fast food approach in general, but the atmosphere is friendly and prices reasonable.

Taverna
(R)S

The first taverna you come to along the beach road is OK, with a nice view of the beach and lots of shade. The menu is of the 'point at a picture' variety, and the vakalaos – cod fried in batter – wasn't anything special, but hot and freshly cooked. Fish, chips, salad and a beer would cost you around 2,000 drachmas.

Map B3   ORMILIA

If you have transport, it's worth making the short, five-kilometre detour inland from Psakoudia to see the traditional village of Ormilia, with its attractive old buildings. There is a monastery there which will admit visitors on Saturday morning from 10 a.m. until midday, and occasionally it may be possible to arrange to attend the Vespers service. As with the **Metochi** in Neos Marmaras, a visit to the monastery can give the visitor a brief insight into the Orthodox religion which is an important and living element in Greek culture and the real lives of the people which seems a world away from the tavernas and bars.

Map C3 **METAMORPHOSI**

One of the more attractive resorts along this stretch of coastline, with a lovely sandy beach where you can find shade under the pine trees. There are a few shops including a supermarket, a bar in the little grassy square which looks down on the beach, and a taverna under the Golden Beach Hotel.

Voutsas taverna
(R)S *Below Golden Beach neon sign*

Lots of outdoor tables with a good view of the comings and goings in the village as well as of the sea. A good selection of fish that's not too expensive, including red mullet (7,500 per kilo), 'flatfish' at assorted prices, swordfish 950 and lobster 10,500 drachmas per kilo. The stuffed squid – with soft feta and lots of flat parsley – is 700 and very tasty, and souvlakia and lamb chops, with piles of fresh chips seemed to be going down well with the Greek customers.

Metamorphosis Bungalows
(H)M

This is a comparative rarity in Halkidiki in that it's an apart-hotel, giving you the option of having all your meals out or preparing them yourself if you prefer. The one-bedroomed apartments have a fridge and cooking rings. The complex is purpose-built, but nicely designed, with low, white buildings and red-tiled roofs set in attractive gardens. Facilities include a mini-market, two pools, with a bar and à la carte restaurant and tennis courts. The accommodation is simple, and conveniently close to the beach and the centre (small as it is!) of Metamorphosis. Nice for those who don't want a huge hotel but prefer more facilities than a room-only deal.

Map C3 **NIKITI**

Just after you pass the sign for Nikiti, there's a left turn which goes up to the old village which has some pretty old houses and a couple of tavernas along the main street. Towards the top, on the left, there's a ceramic and pottery shop which is a bit different from the usual 'Greek art' shops you find in most seaside resorts. There's quite a pleasant stretch of beach down in the resort of Nikiti, with a few bars and the odd taverna. However, it's not very lively outside July and August when the Greeks visit, and has a rather closed feel about it at other times.

After Nikiti, you turn down into the peninsula of Sithonia proper, and the scenery gets even more beautiful. The road round the peninsula climbs quite steeply at times, then sweeps down towards the sea through thick forests. It really is one of the loveliest landscapes in Greece, and well worth a trip, if only for a day.

Map C4 NEOS MARMARAS

Originally a small fishing village of about 300 souls, Neos Marmaras has expanded dramatically over the last thirty years. Its normal population of about 4,500 swells to over 30,000 at the height of the summer season. This results in a fair amount of chaos, especially in the evenings, when frustrated drivers hoot frantically to try and force a path through the people spreading out from the bars into the streets. Nevertheless, it remains good humoured most of the time, and although undoubtedly livelier than most other resorts in Sithonia, Marmaras is still a friendly and relaxed place. There's quite a nice beach at the quieter end of the village towards Porto Carras – fine shingle and trees providing shade when you want it, but no sunbeds or watersports. All along the main street you'll find plenty of shops, selling the usual range of beach goodies, relatively cheap and cheerful clothes, jewellery and leather goods. Belts are good value, and the handbags are reasonably priced but not particularly stylish. The jewellery is mostly gold, and inclines to the ornate. Marmaras is a good place to buy picnic food, fruit and cold drinks, with several supermarkets to choose from and a baker – look for the Artos sign off the main street.

Bugatsa café
(R)S

A treat not to be missed is bugatsa – a filo pastry concoction filled with either confectioner's cream or cheese and served warm. The best place to sample this is the simple self-service café which also serves loukoumades, which are like tiny doughnuts dripping with honey and sprinkled with cinnamon. The café is in the little square behind the jetty where the water taxi from Porto Carras usually docks, four doors to the right of the Zig-Zag bar. There are a few outdoor tables under a white

The lively village of Neos Marmaras.

corrugated awning with just a handwritten sign in Greek. It doesn't look much, but it really is worth at least one visit. You go to the counter and ask for what you want – the bugatsa is then cut from a large piece and weighed and chopped into bite-sized chunks before it is served. The cream version is sprinkled with cinnamon and icing sugar and utterly mouthwatering. You can eat there or take it away. There's an unusually good choice of coffee, and the capuccino is like the real thing, which is pretty rare in Greece. Alternatively, there are cold drinks and beer (light and fizzy) on draught, which seemed to be going down well with Scandinavian holidaymakers, so presumably it's good.

For a brief glimpse into the religious tradition of Greece, it's possible to visit the **Metochi Agiou Grigoriou**, an offshoot of the Athos monastery of St Gregory. Walk to the Porto Carras end of the main street, following, ironically enough, signs to the Summer Loft disco. Along the street which leads back up the main coast road, next to the bar Anonymo, you'll find the gate into the Metochi. Ask for Kyrios (Mr) Kyriakos, and he will unlock the two tiny churches, one of which contains a miracle-working icon of the Virgin Mary. Young women who have been unable to conceive come to kiss the icon and pray for the Madonna to make them fertile. There are several other very interesting icons from the monastery in Athos, albeit a tiny fraction of the treasures which can be seen by those lucky enough to visit the Holy Mountain itself.

Anyone interested in exploring further afield will find several buses a day from Marmaras to Thessaloniki and a few in the other direction to Sarti. You can also get Flying Dolphin hydrofoils to Pefkohori on Kassandra peninsula, and to the islands of Skiathos, Skopelos, Alonisos and Skyros. Details and tickets from Moudania Tours, just up the steep side street behind the square. The taxi rank is behind Dionysos taverna.

Along the road behind the beach, you'll find several small tavernas in a row. They're nothing special, and serve the usual selection at reasonable prices, but fine if you want to eat away from the bustle and crowds.

Dionysos taverna
(R)S

A largish taverna immediately on your left as you come off the main jetty. Plenty of tables overlooking the sea but inclined to be chaotic in high season, and especially at weekends when it is very popular with Greek customers. You may have to be a bit assertive to get attention, and it's a good idea to order everything you want at once, or you may have trouble regaining the waiters' attention. The fish is good, but on the pricey side, otherwise it's the usual selection at reasonable prices.

Taverna Pefka
(R)S

Taverna Pefka – meaning pines – is in a lovely position on the hill overlooking the sea and facing the sunset. You'll find it on the path that goes from behind the large neon Poseidon sign, along the cliff path round the bay. There are some more interesting items on the menu – such as saganaki (fried kephalotiri cheese triangles), okra or lady's fingers stewed with tomatoes and oil, swordfish and fresh sardines in tomato sauce. It has small green lamps, and white fairy lights among the pines, and the service is friendly and efficient. When I was there on a July evening, there seemed to be more staff than customers, perhaps because it's a little out of the way, but I think it is worth seeking out. Expect to pay around 3,000 drachmas for an average meal with beer.

Pizza Risa
(R)S

There are pizza places aplenty, but this one at the Porto Carras end of the main road cooks them in the traditional Italian way in an open, wood-fired oven. Worth a visit if you want a change from Greek food.

Map C4   **PARTHENONAS**

Along the main road between Neos Marmaras and Porto Carras you'll see a sign pointing inland to this delightful village. It's five kilometres up an unmade road (due to be asphalted in 1995), full of twists and turns through woods and olive groves. Once a thriving community, the village was abandoned some years ago by the residents who moved en masse to the coastal village of Neos Marmaras where the living wasn't quite so hard. Now many of the traditional stone houses are gradually being restored, and new window boxes and gardens are being planted all round them. The village still does not have mains electricity or a direct piped water supply, although this too should come soon. The views down over the countryside to the coast are truly spectacular, and you can see the occasional tiny car moving silently far below, while all you can hear is the buzzing of insects and the odd goat bell.

Once you've explored the village, make sure you visit the lovely traditional taverna run by Mr Paul Karapas.

Paul's taverna
(R)M   *0375 71 349*   *Open from around mid-May to early October*

During the day, you can sit at the wooden tables and look out through the trees to the beautiful view, or pass the time chatting with Paul, who's a fount of fascinating stories and quite a character. Formerly cook to the late John Carras (see below), Paul, who lived in the USA for many years, is the perfect host. If you feel like having lunch, he'll list what he has available and tell you to take your time deciding – 'you have until 3 a.m.!' Mostly, it's salads, including a particularly nice one made of beans, while later on there's souvlaki, village sausages and the like, plus the usual salads and starters. Although the food is good and reasonably priced, it's not the main reason the taverna is so popular. In the evenings, the scene is lively, with Mr Paul offering his services to teach his customers all kinds of Greek dancing ('Syrtaki in three minutes!') or even the tango. No one is pressed to take part – those who want to can enjoy their meal in peace or just watch the action. Your only problem might be getting there and back if you don't have transport of your own, but if you're really stuck, phone Mr Paul for advice.

Map C4 **PORTO CARRAS**

About halfway down the east coast of Sithonia is the purpose-built holiday development called Porto Carras. It was the creation of the late John Carras, who bought the land in the mid-sixties from the Athos monastery of St Gregory. The site itself is stunning, with the slopes of Mount Meliton rising up

Exploring the peaceful coves on a windsurfer.

behind the beaches covered not only with pines, almond and citrus trees, but also with the vines which produce the internationally renowned Carras wines. There are three large hotels – the Sithonia Beach, the Meliton and the Village Inn (see page 109) – none of which is particularly pleasing to look at but which offer a wide range of facilities. The Meliton overlooks the marina, where there are some very smart yachts moored, and from where you can pick up the regular kaiki (water taxi) service for 300 drachmas to the nearby village of Neos Marmaras just a few minutes across the bay.

On the beach at Porto Carras, you'll find a wide choice of watersports, including parasailing, windsurfing and motor boats for hire. You can also hire sunbeds and umbrellas and the sea is beautifully clear and clean. The main beach gets fairly crowded during the high season, and if you have the energy (or a car or bike) it's worth taking off to one of the tiny pine-fringed coves to the south of the main resort area.

Cars are only allowed along the first stretch of the track – or you can take the shuttle fun bus which links all the landmarks in the resort – but after that, it's bikes and walkers only. You won't find any sunbeds or other facilities, but pine trees shade the beaches and there are rarely many people about. The marina area is where you'll find shops, bars and cafés, and in the evenings, the excellent Ambelos fish taverna (see below). In the high season, there's also a special wine tasting centre open, in addition to the all-year-round one up on the main road going towards Porto Koufo. You can sample the very good wines made here, and learn something of the history and methods of the vineyard – started by the late John Carras and now world famous.

For the energetic, Porto Carras can offer tennis, golf and horse riding – you'll see the signs on the main road into the resort. Because the whole development is privately owned and run, you'll see a gatehouse with a bar that can be lowered over the road as you enter the resort, and a similar arrangement on the track behind the coves. No one is going to ask you your business, however, and you can just pass through, usually without even stopping. The whole place has been carefully planned and is immaculately maintained with very high standards, but the downside of all that is that it can seem a bit sterile for some tastes.

A more common complaint from people staying in the resort, however, is that prices, especially for drinks, are somewhat steep compared with other places in the area. However, as the management point out, you wouldn't expect to shop at Harrods and pay Tesco prices. This is one of the reasons why many people choose to take the water taxi trips to

Neos Maramaras, particularly in the evenings for an after-dinner drink or to stock up on bottled water or supplies for a picnic lunch. Another reason may be the fact that the various cafés and restaurants open and close at particular times – unlike tavernas almost anywhere else in Halkidiki, where'll you find some customers having breakfast, others lunch and yet others just a drink all at the same time. Some people might miss the friendly semi-chaos you find elsewhere, while to others this would be a positive point.

Some of the facilities are not available after the end of August – including the two nicest eating places, the Oasis and Ambelos. But for those who have the opportunity, both are worth a visit.

Oasis taverna

(R)M *Open June–September, 11 a.m.–7 p.m.*

Take the road towards the coves and you'll find the small converted shepherd's hut with its tables scattered under the trees close to the sea. The Oasis is renowned for its mezedes – a wonderful variety of hors d'oeuvres which are a unique feature of traditional Greek cuisine. The waiter will bring you a tray loaded with that day's selection of cold dishes, and will also tell you what else he has to offer. The idea is that you pick anything you want from the tray, then order anything else you fancy from the list, plus an ouzo at the same time. Then, when the other dishes come, you have a beer to go with them. As well as mezedes such as baby stuffed vine leaves with tzatziki, grilled octopus, fried courgettes or aubergines and prawns saganaki, you can choose more substantial dishes such as meatballs, pasticcio and a delicious mixture of different meats cooked with carrots, peppers, celery and onions called kontosouvi. Most of the mezedes are around 650 drachmas each, with the main dishes ranging from about 1–2,000 drachmas each. It's a wonderful way to while away the hottest hours in the middle of the day in tranquil surroundings which have been carefully planned to resurrect the Greece of fifty years ago.

Taverna Ambelos

(R)L *Open June–September, evenings only*

Situated in the square behind the marina, with tables shaded by pine trees. Traditional Greek cooking from vakalaos (fried cod with garlic sauce), 1,550 drachmas, to pork souvlaki, 1,700, that's a cut above your average taverna. There are some unusual starters too, such as octopus stifado – stewed with onions, 1,650, and spanakotyropitta – little filo pastry pies filled with spinach and cheese, 650. The chef, Mr Vlassis, really knows his job, and can even offer a delicious new Carras wine named in honour of the taverna (1,900 drachmas).

Grecotel Meliton Beach
(H)L

Usually known as the Meliton Hotel, this is a very large (892-bed) five-star establishment with all the comforts and facilities you would expect – including air conditioning and marble bathrooms! It's right on the main beach and next to the marina, and has its own small parade of shops, including several selling designerish clothes at appropriate prices.

The Sangria café next to the marina offers an attractive selection of mezedes during the day and is open 11 a.m.–5 p.m.

Sithonia Beach
(H)L

Even larger than the Meliton, this four-star hotel has 950 rooms and facilities of a very high standard, and it's fully air conditioned. Despite its size, the hotel has a friendly feel, and the reception staff in particular are charming and anxious to be helpful. Although the Porto Carras disco and nightclub is here, guests who like their sleep will be pleased to know that you can't hear a sound from it unless you're actually inside. Again, the hotel is right on the sandy beach, where there's a bar, sunbeds and all the watersports anyone could want. A casino is being built in the hotel over the winter of 1994/95.

L'Orangerie *Open 8 p.m.–12.30 a.m. every evening except Mondays*

This is the Sithonia Beach Hotel's à la carte restaurant, and the name tells you most of what you need to know. Its decor is all trellis and greenery, and the very good food is international in style more than Greek. I enjoyed my meal there, although on a July evening it was pretty quiet and I found the restaurant somewhat low on atmosphere. It could have been in any good hotel anywhere. However, if you want this kind of cooking with excellent service, it could be the place to splash out.

Village Inn
(H)M

Not exactly the converted coach house its name suggests, but a modern three-star hotel with 176 beds and full air conditioning.

Sithonia peninsula

The Marina restaurant
(R)M *Open 7.30 a.m.–10 a.m. (breakfast); 1 p.m.–3 p.m. 8.30 p.m.–11 p.m.*

> This is the Village Inn's à la carte taverna, offering seafood and Greek specialities and lit by oil lamps in the evenings. Unlike some of the others, this is open right through the season. However, if the treatment I received when arriving for a meal (not realising that it was fifteen minutes before closing time) is typical, the reasonable food does not make it worth putting up with the surly service. This is so rare in Halkidiki that it came as quite a shock, and things were little better at breakfast the following morning – when they weren't about to close!

Map D4 **PORTO KOUFO**

> One of the most attractive spots in Sithonia, reached by a stunning road curving through the mountain forests with the deep blue of the sea far below. The bay is almost completely enclosed by green hills, and there's a long, clean coarse sand beach sloping into a deliciously cool clear sea. The village itself is spread along the shore-line, with a supermarket, and three tavernas looking out to sea at the harbour end. The harbour is small but lively, with lots of fishing boats, a few pleasure boats and yachts and the odd speedboat nipping in and out. Yellow fishing nets are spread out to dry on the quay, and the constant comings and goings provide plenty of entertainment for the idle tourist.
>
> As you'd expect, fish is good in all the tavernas, although I was a little disconcerted to see a van draw up at one of them and the driver start to unload boxes of what was apparently frozen squid. Definitely a case of taking coals to Newcastle, I'd have thought.

Taverna Pefkos
(R)S

> This is the middle one of the three tavernas, and had dried mackerel salad for 5,000 drachmas which made an interesting change.
>
> In the furthest one, slightly back from the road, the 'come and look' system operates when you order fish, as it's easier than trying to explain what's available. Even if you don't feel like eating, it's all too easy to while away several hours with a soft drink or a beer, just watching the life of the village.

Map D5   KALAMITSI

From Porto Koufo, the road curves around the end of the Sithonia peninsula, and the views are even more beautiful and spectacular. The smell of herbs and pines growing by the roadside is incredibly strong, and to me always seems to be the essence of Greece. Kalamitsi itself is little more than another long, coarse sandy beach with a couple of bars and tavernas behind, but no less appealing for that. There was actually a coachload of people from the Czech republic sunning themselves on the beach when I was there, having apparently travelled by road. A good place to stop for a swim and a break if you're touring along this part of the coast.

Map D5   SIKIAS

The main beach area is probably one of the least scenic in the region, backed as it is by a large stretch of flat scrub, although it's OK once you get past that.

Five steps to the beach
(R)S

A taverna on the beach run by a Dutch/German couple, with plenty of fish, plus grills and meat stews like kleftiko at pretty cheap prices – about 2,000 drachmas a head for an average meal.

If you head off instead to the right towards Linaraki when you meet the coast road, the prospect is rather more appealing than the main beach. Just about navigable by car, the road gets a bit rough and is very narrow and windy, but it passes through three or four tiny, tree-fringed coves, each with its own little beach taverna offering basic snacks. It's quiet, and the views are very pretty.

Map D4   SIKIA

Just behind the coastal resort, about 2 km from the main road, is the inland village of Sikia. A few enterprising residents have realised the advantages of attracting tourists, and you'll see signs singing the praises of the village supermarket by the turn-off. You see the supermarket on your left as you enter the village, and in the small square there are a couple of bars and fairly basic tavernas where you might like to stop for a drink. It's worth taking a walk to the top of the village where the path meets the lower slopes of the mountains. There are simple village houses with goats, chickens and pretty gardens, and a well where local women collect water in buckets. They seemed surprised to find a Brit venturing so far off the beaten track – apparently German tourists are generally more adventurous. People in the village are friendly and welcoming, and delighted to meet visitors who appreciate the beauty of Sithonia and Sikia in particular.

Map C5 SARTI

They say you can count the monasteries you can see on Athos from Sarti beach, but so far I've never managed this. Either the Holy Mountain was obscured in cloud, or the heat haze was so opaque that I could see nothing but misty outlines of the far peninsula. It doesn't really matter much, however, because Sarti has charms of its own. It's quite a sizeable resort by Sithonia standards. Behind the long beach road curving round the bay, there are shops and cafés among the houses and apartments along several side streets and a couple of smaller roads parallel to the beach.

Sarti has a very long, sandy beach, with a water sports centre at one end, and several tavernas and cafés spread along the road behind.

Galaxias
(R)S

Towards the rocks end, you'll find this large zacharoplasteio offering twelve different kinds of cakes, including the lovely little honey-drenched doughnuts called loukoumades, all at 300 drachmas. To make the choice even harder, there are ten different kinds of ice cream, which come in traditional sundae glasses and are virtually irresistible. There are tables under an awning just behind the beach, where you can sit half the afternoon if you feel like it.

Café Paris
(R)S

A couple of streets back, again at the rocks end of town, the Café Paris is unexpectedly sophisticated. You'll find it in a shady corner of a little square with white canvas directors' chairs and several kinds of coffee.

To be honest, you would be as well picking any taverna you like the look of as the food and prices don't vary all that much from one to another. Few of them have names in English either, but nevertheless, a few suggestions.

Taverna
(R)S

Without any name in English. It's at the far end of the beach road, next to the rocks, and much frequented by Greeks. You sit under an awning which supports a grapevine, and look out to sea. As well as various fish, there are shrimps for 2,200 drachmas, baby stuffed vine leaves (dolmadakia), 500, and veal with potatoes, 1,100 drachmas. If you decide on meatballs, you need to know that what you'll get actually bears much more resemblance to small, spicy sausages, baked in tomato sauce, but very nice all the same. Unless you order fresh fish, expect to pay around 3,000 drachmas a head with wine.

Further along the beach road and practically next to each other are two more reasonable tavernas. One, with a bright red awning, called (in Greek) **Achilleas** and the other **Alexander the Great**. The menus are much as usual and the food is fine, but nothing out of the ordinary.

Sarti Beach Hotel
(H)S

A small, three-star hotel about 1 km outside the village, which is actually on the beach where there are various watersports on offer.

Map C4   **VOURVOUROU**

This is actually a very frustrating place because it's incredibly difficult to find your way to the beach. Basically, this is because Vourvourou is a long, ribbon-like development running along the coast, with masses of trees, and loads of newish private villas built among them. Access to the beach is easiest at Karidi, and from there you can walk along the sands, and you'll also find a small snack bar and supermarket. The beach itself is

Sithonia peninsula

mostly quiet, with a few fishing boats, but not really special enough to justify the effort of getting to it.

Map C4 **ORMOS PANAGIAS**

Small and quite pretty, but a little scruffy, this is the port of Agios Nikolaos, the hill town some 4 km inland. There are a few fishing boats moored, and excursion boats to see the Mount Athos coastline, but it doesn't have a proper bathing beach. There are a couple of bars in the little bay, where you might want to stop for a drink or a coffee.

Local fishermen bring in fresh supplies every day.

Athos peninsula

PIRGADIKIA

Map B4

As the main coast road leaves Sithonia heading towards Athos, you come across the picture postcard fishing village of Pirgadikia. It's little more than a hamlet really, with a charming harbour full of fishing boats and a fish taverna at either end, and a bar and a few shops in between. The beach is nothing special, although you can swim off the rocks at the end. There's also a zacharoplasteio, where you can sample delicious honeyed cakes. The best thing about the tavernas is their position – the Romantza lives up to its name in appearance at least – but you can have reasonably priced standard meals or just sip at a drink while you take in the view. There are some beautiful beaches nearby, at the Assa Maris Hotel, for example.

IERISSOS

Map B4

Ierissos has the air of a town designed for the enjoyment of the people who live there. You'll find Greek families on the beaches, in the tavernas and cafés, the shops and markets and just strolling about the streets. Around 10 p.m., the roads are packed with people walking down into the town – to meet and chat, sit in the bars, and generally see and be seen. Sitting in a taverna, you watch the cars stop outside so the driver can have a chat through his ever-open window with his friends at the nearby table. It doesn't actually cause chaos, because there's very little traffic, and what there is is moving very slowly. This is partly because no one is in a hurry, but probably more to do with the fact that Ierissos has its own, built-in traffic calming system – more speed ruts than speed bumps, but the effect is the same.

There's a branch of the National Bank of Greece close to the main crossroads, where a road branches off to the inland village of Gomati. Look for the 'Change' sign. There's also a post office where you can change currency, travellers' cheques and Eurocheques. On the opposite side of the main road by the Gonia (Corner) café, there's a small but busy market – mostly vegetables and fruit, and several kinds of loukoumi (Greek delight), plus a few stalls selling cheap clothes and shoes. In front of the bank there's a small park, shaded with pine trees and with seats along the pathways. At the far end, you find the Parka taverna where you can have a drink and cool down.

Once a year, at the end of June, the town celebrates 'Sailors' Week', culminating in an evening of festivities on the Saturday. There are stalls selling trinkets, candy floss and fast food like corn on the cob on a stick, and a smoking barbecue just behind the beach which sets fire to the grass at regular intervals. Absolutely everyone comes into town, from the very old to babies, and stays to listen to the band singing Greek songs from 10 p.m. until around 1 a.m. It's very much a festival for the local people, although tourists are welcome to join in, but it's not put on for show.

Tourists in this area seem to be mostly German, and few people in restaurants or shops speak much English. Apparently, the area is beginning to attract tourists from Scandinavia, Hungary, and the countries of former Yugoslavia and Russia.

Otherwise, the beach at Ierissos, with its long, clean and fine shingle is attractive, but has no shade or other facilities.

Taverna Josef
(R)S

Taverna Josef is at the end of the road down to the beach from the main crossroads (signposted 'Beach') on the right-hand side. There are several pleasant outdoor tables and Greek music playing not too loudly in the background. It offers the usual printed menu, with a few extras pencilled in. You might have to try a bit of sign language as the staff don't have a lot of English, but they're friendly and anxious to help. As well as offering fresh fish, with your choice depending on what's been caught that day, it does a very good beetroot salad – home-cooked, sweet, and quite different from the vinegary concoction we're used to at home. Also worth trying are dolmadakia – delicious small stuffed vine leaves, filled with slightly sweet, sticky rice flavoured with herbs, served with tzatziki; red sweet peppers cooked with tomatoes, and fasolakia (green beans stewed in oil – much nicer than it sounds). With a basket of good fresh bread and half a bottle of red wine, you can expect to pay around 3–4,000 drachmas per person. A can of aerosol stain remover was produced with a flourish when I managed to upset a glass of red wine over myself – and very effective it was too!

Psarotaverna
(R)S

At the far end of the promenade in front of the beach heading away from Ouranoupolis on the left-hand side. Although the sign means fish taverna, I was told by the owner's charming daughter Maria that they were changing the menu and so didn't have a printed one to show me. Invited to go inside and look, I rejected the neon-lit options pictured over the serving counter which were mostly of the fast food and kebab variety, and three bowls of different kinds of fish were produced from the fridge for my inspection. I chose 'millini', flat silvery fish about twice the size of sardines. I was served four, fried in a light coating with tomato and olive salad and hot crisp chips. With bread and a bottle of Amstel, it was a bargain at around 1,500 drachmas.

Psarotaverna
(R)S

On the other side of the beach road, towards Ouranoupolis, in front of a beach shop called 'Gold'. A good choice of freshly caught fish, depending on the day's catch and sold by weight, plus the usual selection of starters and accompaniments and main courses such as souvlaki and 'bifstecki'. Small fried or grilled squid (kalamarakia) were fresh and crisp and very popular with the Greek families who made up most of the clientele, both at lunch time and in the evenings. With a good Greek salad, bread and a beer, good value at around 2,000 drachmas.

The two hotels in Ierissos, the small D-class Hotel Markos in the centre and the larger B-class Mount Athos do not currently feature in any British tour operators' brochures. However, you might like to have lunch in Mount Athos' waterside taverna, overlooking the fishing harbour, where the food is simple but good, although the service is not speedy. You'll find the hotel about one kilometre outside the town going towards Ouranoupolis.

Map B4 **NEA RODA**

Although there's not a lot to Nea Roda, it has a definite charm of its own. It's little more than a long, fine shingle beach with tavernas, bars and the like behind, with a couple of streets where you'll find the odd supermarket and taverna on the way up to the main road. There are two or three nice tavernas on the promenade behind the beach, where you can sit and watch the sun go down behind the mountains of Athos as you eat your meal.

Taverna Kostakis
(R)S

As well as offering the usual selection which includes souvlakia, 'hamburguetsa' and pasticcio – a Greek version of lasagne made with noodles instead of flat sheets of pasta – there are one or two more interesting dishes to be found. Try mussels (mydia) cooked in a lemony, peppery sauce with pale green peppers and herbs which is from the same family as moules marinières. Aubergines 'toursi' is a cold concoction – they're stuffed with sweet red peppers and onions and dressed with vinegar. Under the heading 'Greek kitchen', you'll find briam – courgettes, tomatoes and potatoes simmered in a tomato sauce, and beans from the oven – white beans baked with tomatoes and herbs – but they're only actually available in July and August when the Greeks come on holiday! Unless you opt for the fresh fish, which is, as always, more expensive, expect to pay around 3–4,000 drachmas per head, including half a bottle of wine.

Taverna Thalassina
(R)S

Like its neighbours at Kostakis, the Taverna Thalassina reserves Greek specialities for July and August. However, it offers a good selection of fish and shellfish – at a price. Fresh shrimps for example, are 9,000 per kilo, but small fish like gavros (similar to whitebait) come cheaper at 900 drachmas for 200 g. There's a good choice of starters at around 4–500 drachmas each. Try fried peppers or pumpkin, fresh anchovies or aubergine imam – stuffed with a lovely tomato and onion mixture. A couple of starters, gavros, Greek salad and a beer make a good value meal at around 2,500 drachmas.

Zacharoplasteio

Just behind the tavernas is a cake and coffee place where you can sample delicious pastries and watch the world go by along with what looks like half the population of Nea Roda.

Alexandros Apartments
(H)M

Actually an apart-hotel on the road from Nea Roda to Tripiti and set back from it into the hills behind. White, low-rise buildings, with accommodation in studios and small apartments, it has tennis courts, a beach bar and its own shop. It is a bit isolated for some people – although the beach is only 200 m away there's nothing much nearby, and you'd need to get the bus into Nea Roda (2 km) or Ouranoupolis (5 km) to find a choice of tavernas and bars.

Map B4   **AMOULIANI**

A couple of kilometres along the road from Nea Roda is the tiny port of Tripiti where you can get the ferry to the island of Amouliani. Outside the small port police office there's a handwritten timetable – but what it actually lists are the arrival times of the boat from the island. In fact the ferry makes the return journey some 15–30 minutes later. Departures are roughly every two hours, starting at 7.30 a.m. through to 8 p.m. The last boat back from Amouliani is at 8 p.m. – but double check these times when you're there as things can change. There's usually someone in the port police office to help, but do ask them to write the times down even if they speak English. I missed one ferry because the helpful port policeman told me it left at 15 minutes after 12 when he meant 15 minutes before! There's a café next door where you can have a drink while you wait. The single fare is 143 drachmas per person, but if you have a car or bike, it's worth taking it with you as exploring the island on foot can be hard going in the heat. It's 1,500 drachmas each way for a car – and you have to drive on backwards. The journey is only 10–15 minutes. In the port on Amouliani, there are a few bars and tavernas – nothing special in themselves but all with good views of the comings and goings in the harbour and across to Ouranoupolis.

A horse-drawn taxi usually meets the incoming ferry, and will take you to one of the beaches. If you prefer to walk, it'll take you around 30 minutes to get to the lovely beach at Alikes – follow the road sign – where there's a campsite and a fish taverna at the far end, with the usual selection of fresh fish, shellfish, salads and so on.

For the more energetic or those with transport, there's an attractive, uncrowded beach and a tiny taverna 5 km from the port at Agiou Georgiou. To get there, you follow the sign to

Vassilis, then turn left just beyond a garish blue and yellow building about 500 m up the hill. The road turns rather rough, but it's negotiable by car at slow speed and the taverna is just beyond the minute white church of Agiou Georgiou. Food is fresh but basic, the view towards the mainland stunning, and the couple who run it very welcoming and chatty – as far as their limited English allows!

Map B5 **OURANOUPOLIS**

By the standards of Halkidiki, Ouranoupolis is quite a large and sophisticated resort, with lots of shops as well as hotels and

The Byzantine tower and pretty water front at Ouranoupolis.

tavernas. Supermarkets and tourist shops open at around 8 a.m. and stay open until around 9–10 p.m. – they don't close for the usual siesta. As well as the standard collection of beach gear shops, it's worth investigating those selling jewellery and very attractive lace and 'broderie anglaise' items – everything from tablecloths to pillow cases and blouses.

In the morning and around midday, coaches arrive carrying holidaymakers who've booked on the widely advertised 'Athos cruises'. Most tour operators run this excursion from your hotel, but if you want to travel independently, you can get timetables and tickets (costing 3,000 drachmas) from the various ticket offices behind the tavernas. For more about the trip itself, see the section on Mount Athos on page 125.

At the jetty and on some of the hotel beaches you can hire small motor boats for 8,000 drachmas a day plus petrol, and there's a water taxi to the islet close to Amouliani for 600 drachmas. The main beach in Ouranoupolis is a long stretch of fine shingle but has no shade or other facilities, and there are small rocks and a bit of weed at the edge. To find sunbeds, umbrellas and watersports you need to head out of the resort along the road towards Ierissos where there are several beaches attached to hotels with everything from windsurfing to parasailing available.

Hotel Theoxenia
(H)M

2.5 km outside the village, the Hotel Theoxenia is a medium-sized, very comfortable hotel with a fine shingle beach that's reached by a tunnel under the road. There's an à la carte taverna with mostly Greek food, and the hotel is fully air-conditioned.

Hotel Eagles Palace
(H)L

Set among trees on the hillside above the sea, around 4 km outside the resort. This is a relatively large four star hotel with watersports on the beach, tennis courts and bikes for hire. It has a beach bar, garden café and a taverna by the pool, and lovely views out to sea and the island of Amouliani. There's nothing much nearby, but the hotel runs a courtesy bus for a small charge into Ouranoupolis three times a day, or you can get the ordinary bus on the main road. A special attraction is a trip by sea to see the monasteries of Mount Athos on the hotel's own cruise boat – around 4,500 per person.

Philoxenia Hotel
(H)S

> A small, low-rise hotel just at the edge of the village, about 900 m from the centre. It's an attractive building, with a red-tiled roof and plain wooden balcony rails, ranged around a small garden and a terrace with views out over the sea. Simple but friendly and just a short walk from the beach.

Hotel Makedonia
(H)S

> With just fifteen rooms, this family-run establishment looks more like a large house than a hotel, with an attractive terrace/café in front on the ground floor and a breakfast room. It's close to the centre of town, but not near enough for you to be bothered by noise – not that that's much of a problem in Ouranoupolis anyway.
>
> At the other end of the resort, past the Athos taverna (see opposite page), is the start of one of the marked walks planned and signposted by the Halkidiki Hotel Association.
>   There is a long row of tavernas, bars, ice cream parlours and the like starting just behind the Byzantine tower and running along behind the harbour area. The coffee and cake place a few yards on advertises home-made ice cream. I couldn't resist the kadaifi ice cream which turned out to be a finely spun shredded wheat concoction soaked in honey and filled with walnuts and topped with creamy white ice cream. In the end I had to admit defeat and leave a little, but it was delicious.
>   There's not a great deal to choose between the tavernas, but the following are the ones I liked best.

Taverna Paralia
(R)S

> Generally known as Lemoniades, the Taverna Paralia is one of the biggest and most popular tavernas, with the Greeks as well as with foreign tourists. The service is unusually fast, and the food is fresh and nicely presented, as well as being good value for money. Plenty of fish and excellent shellfish – the lobster my neighbours were eating at the next table looked particularly good although it's never cheap. Menu standards such as mini stuffed vine leaves (dolmadakia) and Greek salad were above average – the latter featuring hard-boiled eggs and other extras besides the usual ingredients. Around 2–3,000 drachmas a head.

Psarotaverna
R)S

> Apparently nameless, it's the last one you come to furthest from the jetty and customers when I was there included local crew members from the various boats in the harbour who presumably preferred it to the alternatives. Most of them opted for the fresh fish, including swordfish, cod, sole and dorado. White beans baked with tomatoes in the oven were available, even though the Greek tourist season hadn't properly started. You can have a light meal of various salads and beans for about 2,000 drachmas, but the fish is, as everywhere, more expensive and sold by weight.

Kritikos taverna
R)M

> This isn't actually in the main row of tavernas, but just around the corner to the right about half-way along. It specialises in fish, and is therefore more expensive than the others, but a good bet if you feel like splashing out a bit. Ask what's available, and they'll either explain or maybe take you to the kitchen for a look – it will depend on what's been caught that day. Around 3–4,000 drachmas, depending on your choice.

Athos taverna
R)M

> You'll find this at the other end of town. Walk along the main beach road up the hill away from the tower and past the coach park on your left. The taverna is perched on the top of the hill, and enclosed with trees and flowers, through which you can just see the sea. Many tour operators use it for their 'Greek evenings', when clients pay a set sum for a help-yourself buffet and wine and musical entertainment. Interestingly, they tend to seat British and German customers on opposite sides of the restaurant, with Greeks scattered in between, but you don't have to conform if you don't want to! In any case, you can visit it independently, even on Greek nights, and choose from the normal menu. There are some slightly different starters and salads, such as tomatoes grilled with oregano and oil, aubergines stuffed with feta and garlic, grilled potatoes with garlic butter and white bean salad – all between 300 and 500 drachmas. Fish soup is good, and they also serve the wonderful fasolada – a bean soup crammed with vegetables, for 1,500 and 700 drachmas respectively. Interesting options among the fish are cod with garlic sauce (2,500 drachmas) and

swordfish 2,500. You get live music on bouzouki and guitar thrown in, and a complementary fruit salad to sweeten the bill-paying. There's a certain amount of fooling around with full wine glasses balanced on the singer's head, simple coin tricks to amuse the children and a bit of amateur Greek dancing encouraged. However, the night I was there, it was a one-man-band and didn't get over the top and unwilling participants were left to eat in peace and watch if they chose.

Map A4 STRATONI

Heading north along the coast road from Ierissos, you come next to the village of Stratoni. It has a couple of beach bars, but the beach is spoiled by a quarrying operation at one end. It's probably not worth making a special trip there, but if you're taking the mountain road to the inland villages (see page **00**) or Thessaloniki, the route from Ierissos to Stratoni is stunningly beautiful. The first part is lined with tall flowering pink and white shrubs then climbs through the forest, with a lovely scent from the pines.

Map C6 MOUNT ATHOS (AGION OROS)

Unless you are one of the few travellers who have managed to get an official permit from the appropriate government ministry to cross the border into the monks' republic, you will have to be content with what you can see from the coast of Sithonia or the boat excursion. An Edict (or 'Chryssobulo') issued in 1060 AD by the Byzantine Emperor Constantine Monomahos laid down strict conditions as to who might be admitted, and forbade females from ever crossing its border. Adult males who are Greek citizens are allowed into Athos, and many local fishermen claim to have been there often. The other people who pay regular visits are firemen, as fire is an ever-present hazard in the acres of forest which cover most of the mountain. Occasionally, you may see flashes of red lighting the sky over the Holy Mountain as you watch from a taverna in Nea Roda or Ierissos – a spectacular but very sad sight.

The first monks had begun settling on the wooded, mountainous peninsula in the ninth century, and the first monastery, Megistis Lavras, was founded in 963 AD by Athanassios the Athonian. Today, the number of monasteries is fixed at twenty; seventeen of them are Greek Orthodox, one

Mount Athos today is home to around 1,700 monks.

Russian (St Panteleimona), one Serbian (Helandariou) and one Bulgarian (Zographou). Until about twenty years ago, the number of monks on Athos had been in decline, but since the 1970s, there has been something of a revival. There are around 1,700 monks, and the average age is around forty. The majority of monks are based at one of the monasteries, but there are also fourteen smaller communities linked to individual monasteries, plus a number of 'huts' and 'seats' housing two or three and one monk respectively, and hermitages in isolated caves and and rocky outposts. Anything which the monks need which they cannot produce themselves arrives by boat at the tiny port of Dafni, which you'll see on the boat trip, and which has its own police station and customs house.

Interestingly, time on Agion Oros runs according to the Julian calendar, abandoned by most of western Europe in favour of the present-day Gregorian calendar during the sixteenth century. This means that dates in the monastic republic are ten days behind the rest of us – which presumably seems more significant to us than it does to the monks themselves.

Even the most unimaginative tourist would find it hard to resist the sense of timelessness and the unchanging nature of the monastic life even when seeing Athos from a modern motor boat 500 m offshore. You really do get a strong sense of another world where life remains much as it has been for the last 1,000 years.

The trip down the east coast of Athos from Ouranoupolis takes about an hour and a half, and it's some 20 to 30 minutes before you see the first actual monastery.

Zographou monastery is 160 m above sea level. It is said that there was a monastery on this site in the ninth century, but it was burned by the Catalans at the beginning of the fourteenth century. Renovation began in 1502, and the buildings have been added to continuously since then.

Constamonitou monastery with its stunning red roofs is next to come into view, 200 m above sea level. There are various different traditions as to its origin, but it too was burned by the Catalans in the fourteenth century, before being rebuilt. More building took place in the nineteenth century, with help from such diverse sources as the wife of Ali Pasha and Russia.

Dohiariou monastery is built on a wooded slope not far from the shoreline. It was founded in the eleventh century, but abandoned later because of pirate raids. Later buildings date from the sixteenth century onwards, and the feast of the Archangels Michael and Gabriel is celebrated here on 8 November each year.

Xenophontos monastery celebrates St George on the 23 April, and its real origins seem to be lost in tradition. Whatever its beginnings, it has wall paintings from the sixteenth century, and more recent buildings, including the belfry constructed in 1864.

Panteleimonos monastery is the Russian monastery, conspicuous by its green onion-shaped domes and red-tiled roofs. In the mid-nineteenth century it housed as many as 2,000 monks, but now there are only a few, and services are conducted in Greek as well as Russian. In the belfry is what is said to be the world's second largest bell which weighs 13,000 kilos and has a diameter of 2.71 m.

Xiropotamou (Dry River) monastery has had a dramatic history, having been destroyed or partially burned and rebuilt several times since its origins in the late tenth century. It

The onion domes of the Russian monastery of Panteleimonos

commemorates forty saints, and has among its many treasures four pieces of wood from the True Cross. In the latest disaster to strike the community, part of the south wing was burned in 1969.

Simonas Petras monastery – after you've passed the port of Dafni, you catch your first glimpse of this astonishing monastery. The buildings we can see now, perched perilously on top of a cliff 230 m above the sea, date from 1891, when the monastery was rebuilt after being burned down for the second time. There is a story that a monk helping with the original construction in the fourteenth century fell off a scaffold and down into the ravine below. However, his faith was so strong that he landed at the bottom without a scratch.

Grigoriou monastery was another victim of fire when the original fourteenth century building was burned down in 1761. The present buildings are a spectacular sight, rising out of the rocks right on the sea.

Dionysiou monastery this fortress-like structure watches over the sea from its site 80 m up on top of a great expanse of rock. The great central tower was once actually a watch tower and dates from the sixteenth century.

St Paul's monastery is the last monastery on the western coast, and although its origins stretch back to the beginnings of the monastic community, it was restored after burning by the two Serbian monks who bought it in 1360.

You get a second glimpse of all the monasteries on your return journey, but the boat stays further out from the coast so you won't see them so well.

Bus Timetables

Peninsula of Kassandra

Route

...oniki	7.30	9.00	9.30	11.30	13.30	15.30	17.00	18.00
...a Moudania	8.20	9.50	10.20	12.20	14.20	16.20	17.50	18.50
...a Potidea	8.30	10.00	10.30	12.30	14.30	16.30	18.00	19.00
...a Fokea	8.40	10.10	10.40	12.40	14.40	16.40	18.10	19.10
...itos	8.50	10.20	10.50	12.50	14.50	16.50	18.20	19.20
...llithea	8.55	10.25	10.55	12.55	14.55	16.55	18.25	19.25
...iopigi	9.05	10.35	11.05	13.05	15.05	17.05	18.35	19.35
...lihrono	9.15	10.45	11.15	13.15	15.15	17.15	18.45	19.45
...nioti	9.20	10.50	11.20	13.20	15.20	17.20	18.50	19.50
...fkohori	9.25	10.55	11.25	13.25	15.25	17.25	18.55	19.55

Route

Pefkohori	8.15	9.30	11.30	13.45	15.45	18.00	19.00	20.00
Hanioti	8.20	9.35	11.35	13.50	15.50	18.05	19.05	20.05
Polihrono	8.25	9.40	11.40	13.55	15.55	18.10	19.10	20.10
Kriopigi	8.35	9.50	11.50	14.05	16.05	18.20	19.20	20.20
Kallithea	8.45	10.00	12.00	14.15	16.15	18.30	19.30	20.30
Afitos	8.50	10.05	12.05	14.20	16.20	18.35	19.35	20.35
Nea Fokea	9.00	10.15	12.15	14.30	16.30	18.45	19.45	20.45
Nea Potidea	9.10	10.25	12.25	14.40	16.40	18.55	19.55	20.55
Nea Moudania	9.20	10.35	12.35	14.50	16.50	19.05	20.05	21.05
Saloniki	10.10	11.25	13.25	15.40	17.40	19.55	20.55	21.55

Route

...oniki	5.40	8.00	10.00	12.00	14.00	16.00	19.00
...Paulos	6.05	8.25	10.25	12.25	14.25	16.25	19.25
...a Kallikratia	6.10	8.30	10.30	12.30	14.30	16.30	19.30
...lata	6.17	8.37	10.37	12.37	14.37	16.37	19.37
...eohoria	6.22	8.42	10.42	12.42	14.42	16.42	19.42
...a Triglia	6.30	8.50	10.50	12.50	14.50	16.50	19.50
...grafou	6.35	8.55	10.55	12.55	14.55	16.55	19.55
...nissiou	6.40	9.00	11.00	13.00	15.00	17.00	20.00
...a Moudania	6.45	9.05	11.05	13.05	15.05	17.05	20.05
...a Potidea	6.55	9.15	11.15	13.15	15.15	17.15	20.15
...a Fokea	7.05	9.25	11.25	13.25	15.25	17.25	20.25
...tos	7.10	9.30	11.30	13.30	15.30	17.30	20.30
...llithea	7.15	9.45	11.45	13.45	15.46	17.45	20.45
...ssandria	7.20	9.50	10.50	13.50	15.50	17.50	20.50
...opigi	7.35	10.05	11.05	14.05	16.05	18.05	21.05
...lihrono	7.45	10.15	11.15	14.15	16.15	18.15	21.15
...nioti	7.50	10.20	11.20	14.20	16.20	18.20	21.20
...fkohori	7.55	10.35	11.35	14.35	16.35	18.35	21.30
...tiouri	8.05	10.45	12.45	14.45	16.45	18.45	21.45

Route

Patiouri	5.45	9.00	11.00	13.00	15.00	17.00	19.55
Pefkohori	5.55	9.10	11.10	13.10	15.10	17.10	20.05
Hanioti	6.00	9.15	11.15	13.15	15.15	17.15	20.10
Polihrono	6.05	9.20	11.20	13.20	15.20	17.20	20.15
Kriopigi	6.15	9.30	11.30	13.30	15.30	17.30	20.25
Kallithea	6.25	9.40	11.40	13.40	15.40	17.40	20.35
Kassandria	6.30	9.45	11.45	13.45	15.45	17.45	20.40
Afitos	6.40	9.55	11.55	13.55	15.55	17.55	20.50
Nea Fokea	6.45	10.00	12.00	14.00	16.00	18.00	20.55
Nea Potidea	6.55	10.10	12.10	14.10	16.10	18.10	21.05
Nea Moudania	7.05	10.20	12.20	14.20	16.20	18.20	21.15
Dionissiou	7.10	10.25	12.25	14.25	16.25	18.25	21.20
Zografou	7.15	10.30	12.30	14.30	16.30	18.30	21.25
Nea Triglia	7.20	10.35	12.35	14.35	16.35	18.35	21.30
Eleohoria	7.28	10.43	12.43	14.43	16.43	18.43	21.38
Silata	7.33	10.48	12.48	14.48	16.48	18.48	21.43
Nea Kallikratia	7.40	10.55	12.55	14.55	16.55	18.55	21.50
Ag. Paulos	7.45	11.00	13.00	15.00	17.00	19.00	21.55
Saloniki	8.10	11.25	13.25	15.25	17.25	19.25	22.20

Route

...loniki	6.45	11.00
...a Moudania	7.35	11.50
...a Potidea	7.45	12.00
...a Fokea	7.55	12.10
...tos	8.05	12.20
...llithea	8.10	12.25
...ssandria	8.15	12.30
...viri	8.25	12.40
...urka (Strand)	8.35	12.50
...ssldi	8.45	13.00

Route

...oskidi	11.10	13.10
...urka (Strand)	11.20	13.20
...viri	11.30	13.30
...ssandria	11.40	13.40
...llithea	11.45	13.45
...tos	11.50	13.50
...a Fokea	12.00	14.00
...a Potidea	12.10	14.10
...a Moudania	12.20	14.20
...loniki	13.10	15.10

Route

Saloniki	9.00	13.00	17.30
Ag. Paulos	9.30	13.30	18.00
Nea Kallikratia	9.35	13.35	18.05
Silata	9.45	13.45	18.15
Eleohoria	9.50	13.50	18.20
Nea Triglia	9.55	13.55	18.25
Zografou	10.00	14.00	18.30
Dionissiou	10.05	14.05	18.35
Nea Moudania	10.10	14.10	18.40
Nea Potidea	10.20	14.20	18.50
Nea Fokea	10.30	14.30	19.00
Afitos	10.40	14.40	19.10
Kallithea	10.45	14.45	19.15
Kassandria	10.50	14.50	19.20
Siviri	11.00	15.00	19.30
Fourka (Dort)	11.10	15.10	19.40
Kassandrino	11.15	15.15	19.45
Kalandra	11.30	15.30	20.00
Nea Skioni	11.40	15.40	20.10
Ag. Paraskevi	11.50	15.50	20.20

Route

Ag. Paraskevi	6.50	13.00	17.30
Nea Skioni	7.00	13.10	17.40
Kalandra	7.10	13.20	17.50
Fourka (Dort)	7.20	13.30	18.00
Kassandrino	7.25	13.35	18.05
Siviri	7.40	13.50	18.20
Kassandria	7.50	14.00	18.30
Kallithea	7.55	14.05	18.35
Afitos	8.00	14.10	18.40
Nea Fokea	8.10	14.20	18.50
Nea Potidea	8.20	14.30	19.00
Nea Moudania	8.30	14.40	19.10
Dionissiou	8.35	14.45	19.15
Zografou	8.40	14.50	19.20
Nea Triglia	8.45	14.55	19.25
Eleohoria	8.50	15.00	19.30
Silata	8.55	15.05	19.35
Nea Kallikratia	9.05	15.15	19.45
Ag. Paulos	9.10	15.20	19.50
Saloniki	9.40	15.50	20.20

Peninsula of Sithonia

Route			
Saloniki	11.15	14.15	18.15
Galatista	12.00	15.00	19.00
Ag.Prodromos	12.15	15.15	19.15
Poligiros	12.27	15.27	19.27
Gerakini	12.45	15.45	19.45
Psakoudia	12.50	15.50	19.50
Ormilia	13.00	16.00	20.00
Vatopedi	13.10	16.10	20.10
Metamorphosis	13.20	16.20	20.20
Nikiti	13.35	16.35	20.35
Ag. Nikolaos	14.00	17.00	21.00
Arnenistis	14.20	17.20	21.20

Route			
Arnenistis	8.15	14.30	18.15
Ag. Nikolaos	8.15	14.50	18.35
Nikiti	8.40	15.15	19.00
Metamorphosis	8.55	15.30	19.15
Vatopedi	9.05	15.40	19.25
Ormilia	9.15	15.50	19.35
Psakoudia	9.25	16.00	19.45
Gerakini	9.30	16.05	19.50
Poligiros	9.45	16.20	20.05
Ag. Prodromos	10.00	16.35	20.20
Galatista	10.15	16.50	20.35
Saloniki	11.00	17.35	21.15

Route		
Saloniki	7.30	15.30
Nea Moudania	8.25	16.25
Kalives	8.40	16.40
Gerakini	8.45	16.45
Psakoudia	8.50	16.50
Metamorphosis	9.05	17.05
Nikiti	9.20	17.20
Neos Marmaras	9.40	17.40
Toroni	10.00	18.00
Porto Koufo	10.05	18.05
Sykia	10.35	18.35
Sarti	10.45	18.45

Route			
Sarti	11.30	17.30	
Sykia	11.40	17.40	
Porto Koufo	12.10	18.10	
Toroni	12.15	18.15	
Neos Marmaras	12.35	18.35	
Nikiti	12.55	18.55	
Metamorphosis	13.10	19.10	
Psakoudia	13.25	19.25	
Gerakini	13.30	19.30	
Kalives	13.35	19.35	
Nea Moudania	13.50	19.50	
Saloniki	14.45	20.45	

Route			
Saloniki	9.15	12.45	17.15
Galatista	10.00	13.30	18.00
Ag. Prodomos	10.15	13.45	18.15
Poligiros	10.27	13.57	18.27
Gerakini	10.45	14.15	18.45
Psakoudia	10.50	14.20	18.50
Ormilia	11.00	14.30	19.00
Vatopedi	11.10	14.40	19.10
Metamorphosis	11.20	14.50	19.20
Nikiti	11.35	15.05	19.35
Neos Marmaras	11.55	15.25	19.55
Toroni	12.15	15.45	20.15
Porto Koufo	12.20	15.50	20.20
Sykia	12.50	16.20	20.50
Sarti	13.00	16.30	21.00

Route			
Sarti	5.00	7.00	14.00
Sykia	5.10	7.10	14.10
Porto Koufo	5.40	7.40	14.40
Toroni	5.45	7.45	14.45
Neos Marmaras	6.05	8.05	15.05
Nikiti	6.25	8.25	15.25
Metamorphosis	6.40	8.40	15.40
Vatopedi	6.50	8.50	15.50
Ormilia	7.00	9.00	16.00
Psakoudia	7.10	9.10	16.10
Gerakini	7.15	9.15	16.15
Poligiros	7.33	9.33	16.33
Ag. Prodomos	7.45	9.45	16.45
Galatista	8.00	10.00	17.00
Saloniki	8.45	10.45	17.45

Route			
Saloniki	9.15	12.45	15.30
Nea Moudania	10.10	13.40	16.25
Kalives	10.25	13.55	16.40
Gerakini	10.30	14.00	16.45
Psakoudia	10.35	14.05	16.50
Ormilia	10.40	14.10	16.55
Metamorphosis	10.50	14.20	17.05
Nikiti	11.05	14.35	17.20
Neos Marmaras	11.30	15.00	17.45

Route			
Neos Marmaras	12.30	15.15	18.30
Nikiti	12.55	15.40	18.55
Metamorphosis	13.10	15.55	19.10
Ormilia	13.20	16.05	19.20
Psakoudia	13.25	16.10	19.25
Gerakini	13.30	16.15	19.30
Kalives	13.35	16.20	19.35
Nea Moudania	13.40	16.35	19.50
Saloniki	14.45	17.30	20.45

Peninsula of Athos

Route								
Saloniki	6.00	8.30	10.30	12.30	14.30	16.30	18.30	
Galatista	6.40	9.10	11.10	13.10	15.10	17.10	19.10	
Ag. Prodomos	6.50	9.20	11.20	13.20	15.20	17.20	19.20	
Paleohora	7.00	9.30	11.30	13.30	15.30	17.30	19.30	
Arnea	7.30	10.00	12.00	14.00	16.00	18.00	20.00	
Paleohori	7.35	10.05	12.05	14.05	16.05	18.05	20.05	
Neohori	7.40	10.10	12.10	14.10	16.10	18.10	20.10	
Stagira	7.50	10.20	12.20	14.20	16.20	18.20	20.20	
Stratoniki	7.55	10.25	12.25	14.25	16.25	18.25	20.25	
Stratoni	8.15	10.45	12.45	14.45	16.45	18.45	20.45	
Ierissos	8.25	10.55	12.55	14.55	16.55	18.55	20.55	
Nea Roda	8.30	11.00	13.00	15.00	17.00	19.00	21.00	
Tripiti	8.35	11.05	13.05	15.05	17.05	19.05	21.05	
Ouranoupolis	8.45	11.15	13.15	15.15	17.15	19.15	21.15	

Route								
Ouranoupolis	5.30	7.30	9.30	12.00	14.00	16.00	18.15	
Tripiti	5.40	7.40	9.40	12.10	14.10	16.10	18.25	
Nea Roda	5.45	7.45	9.45	12.15	14.15	16.15	18.30	
Ierissos	5.50	7.50	9.50	12.20	14.20	16.20	18.35	
Stratoni	6.00	8.00	10.00	12.30	14.30	16.30	18.45	
Stratoniki	6.20	8.20	10.20	12.50	14.50	16.50	19.05	
Stagira	6.25	8.25	10.25	12.55	14.55	16.55	19.10	
Neohori	6.35	8.35	10.35	13.05	15.05	17.05	19.20	
Paleohori	6.40	8.40	10.40	13.10	15.10	17.10	19.25	
Arnea	6.45	8.45	10.45	13.15	15.15	17.15	19.30	
Paleohora	7.15	9.15	11.15	13.45	15.45	17.45	20.00	
Ag. Prodomos	7.25	9.25	11.25	13.55	15.55	17.55	20.10	
Galatista	7.35	9.35	11.35	14.05	16.05	18.05	20.20	
Saloniki	8.15	10.15	12.15	14.45	16.45	18.45	21.00	

Index of Places

Afitos 31, 36, 64–70
Agia Paraskevi 21, 22, 36
Agios Giorgios 22
Agios Mamas 34
Agios Nikolaos 22, 24, 34, 39
Agios Pavlos 24
Akanthos 40
Amouliani 19, 25, 119–120
Ano Poli 52
Aristotelous Square 45, 47, 53, 54
Arnea 26, 34, 35, 42
Athos Peninsula 2, 3, 14, 19, 26, 31, 36, 37, 39, 40, 115–128

Cava Carras 23
Chrousso 88–89

Egnatia Odos 45

Fourka 20, 21, 22, 31

Gerakini 31, 99–100
Gomati 39

Hanioti 19, 31, 80–86
Hanth Square 49

Ierissos 115–117

Kalamitsi 31, 111
Kalandra 92–93
Kallithea 14, 15, 16, 22, 70–75
Karidi 113
Kassandra Peninsula 2, 3, 10, 14, 19, 20, 21, 31, 34, 36, 37, 58–99
Kassandrino 22

Kriopigi 19, 21, 22, 31, 74, 75–79
Koumitsa 25, 26

Leoforos Nikis 57
Leoforou Stratou 50
Loutra 89–90

Metamorphosi 31, 101
Meteora 3
Mount Athos 24, 25, 124–128
Mount Katsika 44
Mount Meliton 106
Mount Petros 24
Mount Pavlos 24

Navarinou Square 47, 52, 56
Nea Fokea 38, 59–61
Nea Moudania 14, 19, 34
Nea Potidea 58–59
Nea Roda 26, 34, 37, 117–119
Nea Skioni 22, 90–91
Neos Marmaras 16, 19, 22, 23, 31, 33, 39, 102–105
Nikis 56
Nikiti 22, 31, 36, 38, 101–102

Olinthos 36, 37, 44
Olympiada 31
Ormilia 34, 100
Ormos Panagias 22, 114
Ouranoupolis 25, 26, 31, 35, 38, 120–124

Paliouri 88
Parthenonas 22, 34, 38, 105–106
Pefkohori 19, 31, 86–88
Pella 3

Petralona Cave 36, 44
Pirgadikia 115
Poligiros 34, 39, 40, 41
Polihrono 31, 79–80
Porto Carras xi, 19, 23, 24, 31, 106–110
Porto Koufo 110
Possidi 31, 91–92
Psakoudia 31, 100
Pyrgadikia 31

The Rotonda 48, 52

Sani 20, 21, 31, 36, 38, 61–64
Sarti 31, 112–113
Scala Fourkas 22, 93–97

Sikia 24, 111–112
Sikias 24, 111
Sithonia Peninsula 2, 3, 14, 19, 20, 24, 30, 31, 33, 35, 36, 99–115
Siviri 22, 97–99
Stratoni 124

Thessaloniki x, xi, 1, 2, 3, 13, 14, 15, 16, 32, 37, 45–58
Tripiti 19, 119
Toroni 25
Tsimiski 54, 57
Turtle Island 45

Vergina 3
Vourvourou 113–114